Reindustrialise Britain

Reindustrialise Britain: A Strategy for Wealth Creation

Costas Lapavitsas
Larry Elliott
Doug Nicholls

polity

First published in 2026 by Polity Press Ltd.

Polity Press Ltd.
65 Bridge Street
Cambridge CB2 1UR, UK

Polity Press Ltd.
111 River Street
Hoboken, NJ 07030, USA

ISBN-13: 978-1-5095-7442-1
ISBN-13: 978-1-5095-7475-9 (pb)

A catalogue record for this book is available from the British Library.

Library of Congress Control Number: 2026935006

Typeset in 11 on 13 pt Sabon LT Pro by
Cheshire Typesetting Ltd, Cuddington, Cheshire
Printed and bound in Great Britain by CPI Group (UK) Ltd, Croydon

For further information on Polity, visit our website:
politybooks.com

Contents

Acknowledgements

Thanks are due to Verena Gradinger and Matteo Giordano for outstanding research assistance, making it possible to write this book within very tight time limits, and to Bob Ansell for his work on Artificial Intelligence. George Owers at Polity read the text with meticulous care and made crucial suggestions for improvement. Special thanks, finally, to members of the Socio-Economic Policy Analysis and Research Collective (SPARC) who made vital observations on the content and direction of the book.

Figures and tables

Figures

Tables

Foreword

This book shows how the disastrous neoliberal politics and economics of the last fifty years have warped our economy and made it so weak that it will continue declining without serious and urgent attention.

More importantly, the book makes clear that there are commonsense solutions to our predicament. It very convincingly describes the essential policy initiatives that should be taken to make good out of a very bad job.

The proposals you will find here are big in impact as well as a challenge. But that is exactly why the trade unions and the organisations of civil society must be the key agents in implementing them. Only a democratic movement can develop these ideas, make them common currency, and help implement them. New alignments and social forces have to emerge to create the momentum required for lasting change.

Accordingly, the authors set out devastating criticisms of what is wrong with the British economy and in a unique way describe what needs to be done, focusing on reindustrialisation. They do so in accessible terms designed to be meaningful in education programmes, conference debates and policy formation.

Specifically, Parts I and III make the case for why change is necessary and who must deliver it. But the heart of the book lies in Part II, Chapters 8 to 11, where the authors show in concrete detail how reindustrialisation can actually be delivered – the labour requirements, capital investment, institutional mechanisms and financing. This is not armchair economics but a workable plan. Readers wanting to understand whether the transformation of Britain is genuinely feasible rather than wishful thinking should focus on it.

Reversing the cultural orthodoxies and habits of thought that have spread across the country, along with inequality, declining class solidarity and retreat from production, requires a new approach by the main representative bodies of civil society. This book can play a pivotal role in achieving it.

The trade unions must lead the way, while also broadening their horizons. They must deepen and extend the negotiating agenda in every sector of the economy with a vision of how the country should be run in our shared interests.

The neoliberal political and economic orthodoxies of the last fifty years have failed us. It is high time for our own political economy to make a comeback and this book makes an important contribution to it.

Eddie Dempsey, General Secretary,
Rail Maritime Transport Union.
Fran Heathcote, General Secretary,
Public and Commercial Services Union.
Dave Ward, General Secretary,
Communication Workers' Union.

Summary
Reindustrialise Britain: A Strategy for Wealth Creation

Britain is broken, its economy unbalanced and frayed. We import too much, make too little and underpay millions. This book sets out a measured plan to rebuild wealth creation based on skilled work. Neoliberalism's promise that deregulation would deliver prosperity failed: industry was hollowed out, communities split and child poverty soared. Without change the slide continues.

Deregulated markets have led to stagnating living standards, prioritised finance over production and increased reliance on imports. Corporate power has starved public services and weakened unions, leaving millions in insecure jobs. Faced with these profound economic difficulties, Britain lacks a coherent industrial strategy. Net Zero by 2050, now a legal obligation of UK governments, further complicates the task. Meeting binding climate goals is inseparable from rebuilding production capacity, securing energy and restoring public control over investment and infrastructure.

A disciplined reindustrialisation programme seeks to expand manufacturing and boost productivity. The aim is realistic: to lift manufacturing's weight in the economy to eleven per cent, with clear potential for more. Policies emphasise large-scale training of workers and ensuring fair pay and union rights for all, while adjusting the need to import labour. Public ownership of utilities guarantees reliability and secures key sectors for robust supply chains. A substantial investment wave restructures supply and provides demand, using a majority-public, minority-private model with strict contracts.

The total programme is about £1.41 trillion over ten years, with roughly £850 billion provided publicly and the balance private. That implies raising manufacturing employment by approximately 725,000 by 2035. A Public Investment Bank with sensible leverage provides long-term loans, supported by pensions redirected to UK assets. Public borrowing finances revenue-generating assets, while central bank coordination stabilises costs. Capital controls and managed trade safeguard wages, while Net Zero is integrally incorporated as a priority.

Implementation depends on social mobilisation and political boldness. Revitalised unions and communities are instrumental to success. Repealing restrictive union laws strengthens collective bargaining, empowering workers to shape production. A coalition of workers, youth and communities can connect workplace efforts to housing and environmental goals. Democratic economic control is vital for rebuilding wealth and ensuring genuine international cooperation. Britain can be transformed based on popular and national sovereignty.

Finally, the need for that transformation is evident in the greatly worsening geopolitical environment. Militarism and the threat of war have become a permanent feature of international politics. The war in Iran and Lebanon, which began after we finished this book, once again exposed the fragility of global supply chains. One key lesson from it is that countries must rebuild national economic resilience. For Britain, heavily dependent on imported energy, food and manufactured goods, there is no time to waste. Our reindustrialisation proposals are not simply about domestic wealth creation, but also about creating the social conditions for peaceful international cooperation.

Part I

Damaged Goods – A Diagnosis

1
Neoliberal disaster

Rare is the child who grows up without hearing the story of the emperor's new clothes. It is the tale of how two conmen posing as weavers convince a vain ruler that they can conjure up magnificent garments that are visible only to those with the intelligence to see them. Those who can't are fools. Fearful of being thought stupid, nobody states the obvious until, while parading his finery on a royal procession, a child blurts out that the emperor is walking around stark naked.

Hans Christian Andersen's folk tale has nothing on the web of deceit spun to voters in the West for the past half century. Market forces, they were told, were the secret to a well-functioning economy. Low taxation for the rich would encourage risk-taking and encourage wealth to trickle down from rich to poor. The state was never the answer to any economic problem, but always the barrier to finding a solution. Indeed, any suggestion that the state should have a bigger role in running the economy was rejected on the grounds that those making the case for a more interventionist approach were seeking to return Britain to 'the bad old days of the 1970s'.

Let us be clear from the outset. This book supports nationalisation of public utilities and other productive resources as well as tilting the balance of power in the workplace back in favour of labour. It argues that capital controls and managed trade will be needed to rebuild manufacturing and make growth environmentally sustainable. But it is not an attempt to turn the clock back fifty years. It is a plan for national economic revival in the 2020s and beyond.

The book is a direct challenge to the status quo and the economic thinking that underpins it. This comes in a variety of forms. There is the school of thought that says Britain is now a services economy and it is pointless to change course. Other countries make stuff; Britain's comparative advantage lies in the City of London, accountancy and management consultancy. The point is, however, that Britain cannot rebuild prosperity, reduce inequality, or regain sovereignty without rebuilding its productive base. This means reindustrialisation, not as nostalgia but as recognition of how complex modern economies work. The alternative to rebuilding Britain's manufacturing base is not an economy dominated by highly paid 'knowledge' workers but a low-tech low-paid servant economy in which finance dominates.

There are plenty of people – across the political spectrum – who agree that manufacturing matters, but who nonetheless say the reindustrialisation ship has sailed and that it is too late to change course. But Britain is a rich country, with abundant amounts of untapped talent. It is never too late to change course, especially if a country is on the road to nowhere.

Finally, there are those who say our proposals have merit, but they fail to take into account the power of the financial markets. The short-lived government led by Liz Truss in the autumn of 2022 shows what can happen – and happen quickly – if investors lose confidence and start to sell UK assets. Some modest tinkering with the economy may be permissible; radical change will be vetoed by the threat of a strike by capital.

Clearly, the potential is there for the bond markets to cut up rough if an incoming government is unprepared. That means being prepared for the backlash rather than abandoning ambition and recognising the need for controls on capital. The power of the bond markets is not a force of nature; rather it is the result of political decisions taken since the 1970s. As this book shows, the barriers to taming the bond markets are political not technical.

1.1 The big lie

For decades, the public was told that a hands-off approach to economic policy was not just the best route to modernisation and lasting prosperity but the only way. Only fools would dispute these blindingly obvious truths, which over time came to be accepted as the conventional wisdom by parties of both left and right. The small group of sceptics were advised to take heed of Margaret Thatcher's dictum: you can't buck the market.

It has taken a long time, but these claims have now been exposed for what they always were – myths. After a decade and a half of weak growth, flat-lining living standards, austerity and growing inequality, it is clear that the emperor has no clothes. Liberal economics has failed and globalisation is in retreat. Voters in the West are furious at having been played and at the damage that has been caused.

That damage has been profound. In Britain, there is a sense that the country is broken, that nothing works, and that public services are getting worse despite taxes going up. There is a growing – and visceral – loathing of a political establishment that promises so much yet delivers so little. Put simply, the public have had it with the British political class who seem unable or unwilling to use the tools of the state to drive growth, improve public services and protect communities from the ravages of global capitalism. The world has been here before. As in the 1930s, economic failure has created an ugly political mood, with right-wing populism and fascism on the rise.

Anger has been festering since the Great Crisis of 2007–9 – the moment when it should have become obvious that the emperor was wandering around without a stitch of clothing to his name. If ever there was a time for a reassessment of the policies that had dominated Western nations for the previous thirty years – financial liberalisation, curbs on trade unions, trickle-down economics, the sale of large chunks of the public sector to asset strippers, and the widening gulf between rich and poor – then this was it. What was presented as economic modernisation had led to industrial decay, with too often nothing to replace it.

1.2 The disaster deepens

Disastrously, the opportunity for a political reset was not taken and – in large part due to the low interest rates and money creation delivered by central banks – a form of zombie capitalism staggered on. Until 2009, the Bank of England had never reduced interest rates below two per cent since it was founded in 1694. The Great Crisis saw rates cut to 0.5 per cent – and they remained around that level for the next thirteen years.

Those with financial and other assets benefited from the rising share and property prices generated by cheap and plentiful quantities of money pumped into the economy, while those not so fortunate were told that the money borrowed by the state to bail out the banks after their speculative frenzy had to be repaid. The era of austerity dawned and has yet to be properly finished off.

The vote for Brexit in 2016 was one warning sign of mounting unhappiness with the status quo that should have been heeded. The enthusiasm – short-lived though it was – for Jeremy Corbyn when he became leader of the Labour Party – was another. Elsewhere, the victory of Syriza in Greece in 2015 was a backlash against the virulent austerity demanded by European elites as the price for financial support. Donald Trump's first term as president was only possible because he tapped into the sense that voters in the so-called 'rust belt' of the USA had been abandoned by east and west coast liberals.

That sentiment also helped explain Trump's return to the White House following his victory over Kamala Harris in 2024 – but with one key difference. The cost-of-living crisis that began in 2021 was a fresh blow to living standards following more than a decade of stagnant inflation-adjusted wages across the developed world. In the UK, real wages adjusted for price rises rose steadily in each decade from 1970 to 2007 but then experienced the longest period of stagnation since the Napoleonic wars of the early nineteenth century. In 2023 they were barely higher than they were in 2007.

Recessions are always bad for workers, but the downturn that accompanied the Great Crisis differed from previous slumps. In the early 1980s, for example, the pain was overwhelmingly borne by workers laid off in manufacturing and the level of official unemployment stayed above three million for five years. But for those who stayed in work in the 1980s real wages continued to rise.

In the recession of 2008–9, the pain was more widely shared, with across-the-board cuts in wages and hours for those remaining in employment. The pound fell, leading to higher prices of imported goods. Wages lagged behind, so living standards suffered. Fewer businesses failed and while unemployment rose it didn't reach the levels of the early 1980s and 1990s.

The first half of the 2020s saw the arrival of three separate setbacks that deepened the malaise: a pandemic, a surge in inflation, and the war in Eastern Europe between Russia and Ukraine. This time, however, the mood among workers was less passive than it had been during the Great Crisis. Following the lockdown of much of the economy in 2020 and early 2021, there was a surge in demand as businesses reopened. The number of job vacancies increased sharply, and workers were in their strongest bargaining position in decades. The start of the war in Eastern Europe in February 2022 then pushed up energy prices and gave another added twist to inflation. As was the case during the Great Crisis, there was a sharp drop in real wages but after more than a decade of stagnation workers had had enough. There was a wave of strikes not just in the more heavily unionised public sector but also in the private sector, where union membership is much lower.

1.3 A world in crisis – once capital runs free

Predictions that the development of new vaccines to combat the Covid-19 virus would prove the catalyst for a rapid recovery, and even a new 'roaring twenties', were wide of the mark. Instead, it has gradually become clear that since 2007–9 we have been living through the third major long-term crisis of international capitalism of the past one hundred years.

The first of these – in the 1930s – eventually gave rise to a post-war settlement that embraced a left-of-centre political agenda – full employment, public ownership of key industries, a stronger voice for organised labour, and investment in an expanding welfare state. But the second – in the 1970s – shifted the pendulum in the opposite direction. Ideas that had lain dormant for decades came back to prominence as the long boom after the Second World War ended in recession, rising unemployment, surging inflation and industrial unrest.

The recipe promoted by the re-energised right-wing of the Tory Party was privatisation, curbs on trade unions, a smaller state, and the abandonment of full employment as the over-riding aim of economic policy. Controls on capital, imposed to ensure governments could pursue domestic goals unhindered by speculative attacks, were removed. The early 1980s was an era of rapid financial liberalisation, especially in the UK and the USA.

Western economies – and the UK especially – were hollowed out by de-industrialisation. In 1979, manufacturing accounted for almost thirty per cent of the UK's annual economic output. By 2010 it was down to eleven per cent and it has since fallen further to just over eight per cent. Manufacturing employment has fallen from 6.8m in 1979 to 2.6m, and not since the early 1980s has the UK recorded a trade surplus in goods. Instead, there has been an increasing reliance on financial and business services – the proceeds of sectors such as banking, insurance, management consultancy and the law – to plug the gap.

Britain is not alone in this trend. Several major economies across the world, with the USA in the lead, embraced globalisation and became financialised. Large industrial and commercial enterprises crossed borders, established capacity abroad and traded internationally. Capital flowed to countries where labour was cheap and favourable terms were offered to big business.

As recently as 2004 rich developed nations accounted for seventy per cent of global manufacturing. By the early 2020s that was down to forty per cent. The US share of global manufacturing has fallen from twenty-two per cent to fifteen per cent, while that of China has risen from nine to thirty per cent. By contrast, the financial sector took on a bigger role, filling the gap left by industry's decline. Financialisation grew in leaps and bounds, drawing working people into the arms of the financial system through mortgages and loans.

Letting capital out of its cage permitted an orgy of profit-making and speculation, eventually leading to a third long-term crisis, which came to a climax in the autumn of 2008. The US investment bank Lehman Brothers collapsed and threatened an existential financial meltdown only averted by taxpayer-funded bailouts and, in some cases, nationalisation of banks. The outcome of this third crisis – a crisis of globalised and financialised capitalism – is as yet unknown. Unlike the crises of the 1930s and the 1970s there has been no new settlement, but rather a cobbled-together attempt to return to business as usual.

The 2020s have been a particularly dismal time. Five years ago, when the first reports emerged of a new virus that had its origins in the Chinese city of Wuhan, it was hard to imagine that Covid-19 would have such a devastating impact. Yet, within months the global economy was in lockdown, businesses were shuttered, trade flows had dried up and governments were spending freely to prevent deep recessions turning into something even more catastrophic.

A second Great Depression was just about averted when the pandemic hit in 2020, but half a decade on the long-term effects are acutely felt. As in the 1930s and 1970s, the global economy is suffering a major system breakdown. The failure of ultra-low interest rates, flooding markets with money and budget deficits to jump start sustained and sustainable growth shows that there is only so much that can be done on the demand side of the economy if the supply side persistently under-performs.

Making the situation much worse than the 1930s and 1970s, the systemic breakdown since 2007–9 has been accompanied by a worsening climate and environmental crisis. Global warming is already having a major impact on everyday life and economic activity across the world. The destruction of the natural environment as big businesses criss-cross the planet in search of profits is unprecedented. The global production chains that have been created have a tremendous footprint of greenhouse emissions.

Despite repeated promises by leading governments across the world, none of the targets set at global gatherings have been met. Big business, meanwhile, continues to speak the language of environmental concern regularly 'greenwashing' its activities. Britain, moreover, now operates under a legally binding commitment to achieve Net Zero emissions by 2050. Meeting that obligation cannot be separated from the wider crisis of wealth creation. It will not be achieved without transforming the economy, expanding the role of the public sector and confronting the material constraints, including energy, on which any programme of reindustrialisation depends.

1.4 Labour impoverished

In the years following the Great Crisis the labour market became more precarious, with the rise of the gig economy and a sharp jump in self-employment as those laid off in sectors like construction scratched a living as sole traders. By 2023 half of the NHS trusts were providing food banks for their staff. A report by the House of Commons library showed that the number of workers on zero-hour contracts increased five-fold to one million between 2000 and 2022.

Estimates of the size of the gig economy vary but, according to the TUC, 4.4m workers were engaged in insecure, precarious jobs in 2023 – almost fifteen per cent of the UK workforce. It used to be that child poverty was primarily a feature of households without work but that is no longer the case. In 2026, a third of children are living in poverty and more than half of them come from working households.

Poverty wages are by no means new in Britain. After the rise of neoliberalism, the numbers have been increasing because far fewer workers are members of trade unions or covered by collective bargaining agreements. Under the New Labour governments of Tony Blair and Gordon Brown, tax credits were used as a way of helping those on low incomes make ends meet, but the value of these was cut by the coalition government of Tories and Liberal Democrats after 2010.

Regional policy under the Labour governments between 1997 and 2010 largely consisted of re-cycling the taxes generated by the speculative activities of the City into an expansion of public sector employment. During the premierships of Tony Blair and Gordon Brown, the bulk of the new jobs in the Midlands, the North, Wales and Scotland were in the public sector. Manufacturing jobs continued to be shed, and when the Great Crisis arrived the proceeds from speculation dried up, as did public sector job creation. The regions bore the brunt of the austerity of the early 2010s just as they bore the brunt of the manufacturing wipe-out of the early 1980s.

The growth of low-paid service sector employment has resulted in a marked productivity slowdown, with output per worker only five per cent higher than its 2008 level by 2023. These trends – low pay, precarious work, benefit restrictions, under-resourced public services – have been reinforced by large inflows of immigrant labour within a low-investment, weakly enforced labour market regime that favoured substituting cheap labour for capital. This happened because governments of both left and right expanded labour supply against a backdrop of weak enforcement of labour laws, barriers to collective bargaining and tight public spending controls. Migration functioned as a deliberate strategy by employers, who exploited prevailing labour market conditions, and its patterns often reflected British colonial history. The mechanisms were institutional and brought about through government policy, increasing pressure on British and migrant workers alike.

In the thirty years up until 1994 the number of people leaving and arriving in the UK was roughly in balance but, since then, the numbers arriving have outstripped the numbers leaving. Net migration exceeded 100,000 in every year from 1998 to 2020. It escalated greatly during the first half of the 2020s, reaching more than 900,000 in 2023. As we argue in this book, immigration can be a major asset within a strategy of reindustrialisation. Britain needs skilled workers across a wide range of sectors, and migration can help meet that need. But the benefits of immigration will materialise only if it is integrated into a national plan for the labour force and is linked directly to domestic training and upskilling, while ensuring full labour rights and social integration for migrant workers. No such transformation can take place without firmly opposing the nasty anti-immigrant campaigns fostered by the populist right and the fascist extreme of British politics.

Our plan for industrial renewal seeks to keep the country open and relies – particularly in its early stages – on migrant workers to cope with skill shortages. At the same time, we are clear that the expansion of labour supply under weak enforcement over several decades became a neoliberal instrument serving the interests of big business. The ready supply of immigrant labour allowed employers to substitute low-paid workers for capital investment in a system deliberately structured to make cheap labour preferable to machinery, thus harming productivity growth and further blunting the ability of unions to press for higher wages. A viable industrial strategy requires migrant workers to be treated the same as UK-born workers, with full labour rights and collective protection, because sticking to the past regime merely reproduces the low-wage model. Equality of treatment would boost solidarity and prevent wage undercutting.

High levels of net migration over the past two decades increased the size of the economy as measured by gross domestic product but growth in GDP per head of population – a better measure of success – was weak. This reflects how growth has been organised, not who arrived. Under present institutions built on low investment and weak labour protection, inflows of this scale strain housing, services, and bargaining structures in a country with anaemic growth, stagnant productivity of labour, falling disposable incomes, and sustained pressure on public finances and welfare provision. But treating migrants as the problem mistakes the symptom for the regime that produced it. The target of our reindustrialisation proposal is the regime itself.

What's now required in Britain is a fundamental rebuilding of the economy from the bottom up. This will take time and a programme of reform that goes beyond mere tinkering around the edges. While, in theory, the ideas we suggest in this book could be picked up by any political party, in reality only a party on the broad spectrum of the left is likely to do so. In our view, there are several reasons why progressives need to seize the moment and come up with a cogent and workable plan to sort things out.

1.5 Fundamental change is needed

The first reason is that the malaise shows no sign of coming to an end of its own accord. There is much talk – most notably from meetings of the global elite in Davos – of how technology will ride to the rescue, but little hard evidence that the much-heralded Fourth Industrial Revolution is having a significant impact on growth and investment, or on living standards. Use of artificial intelligence is increasing, but largely without democratic or employment safeguards, and with the financial benefits concentrated in the hands of a few giant US tech companies. The reliance of Britain's AI sector on US investment risks repeating mistakes of the past through a failure to exploit advances in science.

The second reason is that the public demands no less than drastic action. Historically, there is a strong link between the level of support for governments and whether living standards are rising or falling. A key reason for Labour's landslide victory in the 2024 general election was that real incomes were lower than they had been at the 2019 election. It was, though, hardly a ringing vote of confidence since Labour secured more than four hundred seats with just 33.7 per cent of the vote. The message was that the public wanted change but were uncertain whether Labour could or would deliver it.

Labour's record in office has only added to the suspicions that Sir Keir Starmer had a strategy for winning the election but no plan for what to do next. Yet, opinion polls suggested voters – even those who backed the Conservatives – supported stronger protection for workers, nationalisation of public utilities such as Thames Water, and using state support to keep domestic steel plants open. On these, and other issues, including wealth taxes, the British public was to the left of the parliamentary Labour Party.

Without a coherent plan for getting Britain out of its disastrous predicament, Labour will eventually suffer the fate of its sister parties in Germany and France and even the Democratic Party in the USA. But to be successful such a plan must involve the wider labour movement and be more than a top-down, Whitehall-dominated affair.

The third reason for drastic action, then, is that Britain needs a government with much more than a tepid commitment to renewing the economy. Britain calls for a transformation after the historic failure of globalisation and financialisation, and this requires the active support of a wide constituency across the country, particularly the trade unions. The signs from the Labour government so far have been anything but encouraging.

1.6 Wealth creation not speculation

The Thatcher governments changed Britain profoundly not simply because the neoliberal right found flaws in the post-war Keynesian economic model. Rather, they had a programme ready to be rolled out after the 1979 general election. Something equally far-reaching is once again required, because Britain faces a prolonged period of decline unless action is taken without delay.

Decisive and ambitious steps are required to form a wealth creation model that works for more than the top one per cent of the income distribution. Simply rejecting austerity and intervening on the side of aggregate demand is insufficient, and the aim of policy should be boosting true wealth creation by restructuring the economy's supply side. This will require, at the very least: a wave of public investment, a green new deal, a coherent industrial strategy, active regional policy, a more progressive tax system, a sensible and fitting policy on immigration, controls over trade and capital flows, and the return of key utilities and industries to the public sector. Such a transformation of the country is absolutely necessary to achieve the Net Zero aims and to protect the environment.

Wealth creation is not the same as growth. Countries can achieve faster growth by ramping up consumer spending, by importing more than they export, by cutting taxes while selling off chunks of the public realm, by the speculative activities of an over-sized financial sector. That is not wealth creation, although it sums up what has happened in Britain these past forty years.

To be sure, those who have benefited from neoliberal policies will resist ferociously. Above all, the financial sector will fight the return of capital controls tooth and nail, but the case for them has become more powerful in recent years. As Keynes said in his 1933 essay 'National Self Sufficiency': 'Ideas, knowledge, science, hospitality, travel – these are the things that should of their nature be international. But let goods be homespun wherever it is reasonably and conveniently possible and, above all, let finance be primarily national.' After a prolonged period in which Britain has imported far more than it has exported and been at the mercy of international finance, it is time to heed Keynes's advice. Britain needs to control both trade and capital flows as the rest of our book shows.

The fourth reason for drastic action – and why inactivity would be a potentially catastrophic mistake – is that the authoritarian and populist right has already shown that it is prepared to fill any political vacuum. Donald Trump's populism has struck a chord in the USA because he has identified what millions of working-class Americans want: job security, rising real wages and a sense that their children will be better off than they are. Trump, like other right-wing populists, has been adept at filching policies that have traditionally been associated with the left, such as the use of protective tariffs to nurture domestic manufacturing.

Protecting industries while they are in their early and vulnerable stages of development has been part of the successful growth strategies of China, Japan, South Korea and Taiwan. But, for too long, parties of both left and right in the West have used globalisation as an excuse for passivity and retreated into the comfort zone of identity politics. The unbridled globalisation of the 1990s and 2000s proved disastrous and the left needs a plan for an era in which the state can once again actively use tax, tariffs, public procurement and capital controls as the way to shape economic performance.

1.7 Ending the illusion

The pandemic and its aftermath have changed the rules of engagement in Britain and across the West. Ideas that were seen as off limits – such as furlough schemes to pay the wages of temporarily laid-off workers and state aid for businesses – have been rehabilitated. Ideas that had gone out of fashion in the 1980s – such as more power for trade unions and state ownership – are popular once more.

Our argument in this book is that during the past several decades we have witnessed the decline of industry, the weakening of labour, and the hollowing out of democracy feeding the authoritarian right. For decades, there has been a plundering of the real wealth-creating economy and the public realm, both materially and culturally. Meanwhile, the climate and the natural environment became steadily worse as unbridled capitalism took no effective action and merely 'greenwashed' its profit-making. The failure of neoliberalism as an economic ideology and as policy is undeniable. Nation states are making a comeback and not before time. This might well be the last chance to put things right.

The referendum in the UK in favour of leaving the European Union in 2016 was a signal that this agenda – exploitative financialised and globalised capitalism benefiting a small minority – was no longer acceptable to millions of people. The true message of Brexit is that working people deeply resent the neoliberal mechanisms manipulating politics, economy and society in Britain. Far from being a self-inflicted injury, or a hindrance, Brexit broke the spell of presumed impotence in the face of transnational organisations that serve primarily the interests of big business. It provided Britain with the opportunity to use policy tools that have been off limits for the past four decades. It is up to the country to start using them.

Our book begins with an overview of the state of the British and other major economies. It then examines the particular problems Britain faces before proposing a radical and concrete strategy to solve them. The final part of the book argues that the sort of changes we are proposing will be good for workers and the communities they live in but also the climate and the natural environment.

Part I diagnoses how we got here, and Part III explains who must act and how. But the proof that transformation is possible – the detailed strategy showing it can be done – is in Part II, Chapters 8–11. That's where we show our working.

A word of warning is necessary, though. There is a fifth reason for urgent action – the window of opportunity will not remain open indefinitely. At the end of Hans Christian Andersen's story, the emperor decides to continue with his royal progress as if this was the plan all along. Britain cannot afford that.

2
The world in the slow lane

2.1 EU and USA in trouble

Down the years the booby prize of being known as the sick man of Europe has been like pass the parcel at a children's party: everybody has had a turn. In the 1970s the UK and Italy were the front runners; France had its moment in the 1980s; and by the early 2000s it was Germany's go. Pundits were spoiled for choice in the 2010s as the shock waves from the Great Crisis engulfed the southern European countries of Greece, Italy, Spain and Portugal. Germany was again in the spotlight following Russia's invasion of Ukraine in 2022, with its energy-intensive, export-dominated model hard hit by rising gas prices and the retreat of globalisation.

Today, the idea of picking out a sick man of Europe is pointless because it is easier to pick out the countries that could not be so identified. The economic woes affecting Germany and France show that the sickness which initially only seemed to be affecting Europe's periphery has now burrowed its way to the continent's core. There are obvious parallels with the Great Crisis, which had its origins in the financial crises that rippled through developing and emerging market economies in the 1990s before bringing down the global hegemon – the USA – in 2008. Only then were the structural weaknesses of unrestricted capital flows finally recognised. Keeping the global economy afloat in the illusory boom years of the 1990s and early 2000s had only been possible by allowing a debt time-bomb to be planted in the world's banking system. It was only a matter of time before the bomb exploded.

Britain is therefore not alone in facing difficulties. True, Britain's challenge looks more daunting given that it has an etiolated productive sector balanced precariously on an overblown financial sector, but the UK's predicament needs to be put in the context of a collapsing international neoliberal order. Europe is in structural decline and suffering from similar problems to the UK: weak growth, flat-lining productivity, stagnant living standards, a lack of investment in public infrastructure and increasing pressure on welfare spending due to an ageing population. Germany's industrial model has not adapted to the digital age, but the malaise affects the entire EU and has exposed the intrinsic structural problems of the drive for ever-closer union.

The shoring up of the European integrationist 'project' has necessitated growing militarism. Where once the justification for ceding national sovereignty was to avoid a repeat of the wars that devastated Europe in the first half of the twentieth century, the failure of neoliberalism to deliver lasting economic success has required a new rationale: that Europe needs to rearm and be united to face a potential threat from Russia, Iran and China. Having failed to deliver what was promised on growth and living standards, the EU is trying to re-invent itself as a defence pact – as NATO without the Americans. The idea that ramping up defence spending will boost growth is a fantasy, unless – as in the Second World War – it is on a colossal scale. It would also require less spending for the peacetime economy.

The recent growth record of the USA has been superior to that of Europe, especially so in the aftermath of the

Covid pandemic. Up to a point, this comparison is valid in that US companies dominate the technology sector and the USA – together with China – is far ahead of the rest of the world in the development of artificial intelligence. Europe has no equivalent to Facebook or Amazon and has no real idea how to create rivals to the US behemoths.

Yet much of the difference between US and European growth rates is due to America's more relaxed approach to fiscal policy. In short, the US budget deficit has been allowed to grow wider, mostly through borrowing, to support aggregate demand. A large part of that demand – courtesy of de-industrialisation and the outsourcing of production to Asia – has been met from overseas leaving the USA with a chronic trade deficit. But the country has been able to carry the deficit over time because of the unique role of the dollar as the world's leading reserve currency. At the same time, the debt of the US government continued to increase and currently stands at extraordinary levels approaching $40 trillion. How long the leading superpower will be able to maintain this position is unclear, but it will not be indefinitely.

Moreover, a distinction needs to be drawn between US multi-national companies – which have a dominant global position – and the US economy itself. Just as Thatcher fundamentally changed Britain, so Ronald Reagan, aided by then chairman of the Federal Reserve, Paul Volcker, fundamentally changed the USA in the 1980s. Real median wages – adjusted for inflation – have barely risen in the US for half a century, and productivity gains from a growing economy have been largely captured by the top 0.1 per cent of the population.

One thing the USA has been good at, however, is experimentation – being prepared to ditch neoliberalism in a crisis and try something new. The effective nationalisation of Wall Street banks during the Great Crisis, the huge quantitative easing programme that followed and expanded the money supply enormously, Joe Biden's subsidies for green manufacturing in the early 2020s, and

Donald Trump's trade tariffs during his first term in the 2010s but even more in 2025 are all examples of this willingness to break with neoliberal orthodoxy when occasion demands it. Indeed, the stunned reaction by left of centre parties to Trump's announcement of protectionist measures echoed the remark by a former Labour minister when Britain came off the Gold Standard in 1931: 'Nobody told us we could do that.'

2.2 In China it's different

The protracted crisis of neoliberalism has made Western countries sensitive to the threat posed by China, which has followed an entirely different growth model. China was peripheral to the financial crisis of 2008 and – courtesy of years of trade surpluses – alone had the firepower to haul the global economy out of recession.

Contrary to the predictions of its many Western critics, China has not remained a low-cost hub for the production of cheap manufactured goods. On the contrary, it has steadily climbed higher in advanced manufacturing. It has, for instance, cornered the market in solar panels and is a world leader in affordable electric vehicles. Since 2017 the price of Chinese electric vehicles (EVs) has fallen by fifty per cent, while EV prices have risen by 12.5 per cent in the US and by seventeen per cent in the EU. China has achieved this not by adhering to neoliberal prescriptions but rather by developing a model in which the state provides subsidies to support the electric vehicle sector while encouraging rival EV producers to compete with each other. This approach to industrialising is common in East Asia.

For at least the past fifteen years, Western pundits have argued that China's investment-led model of growth was headed for collapse, but this hasn't happened either. To be sure, China faces major challenges as it seeks to make its economic model more consumer-driven and to tackle the enormous excesses of its real estate sector, but it is still growing at five per cent a year – a performance that the developed countries of the West cannot but envy. Britain is in such a deep hole that now is the time to look at things afresh, including learning from how East Asian countries have systematically planned and nurtured export sectors of their economies, while Western countries have allowed theirs to wither. Before we explore in depth the alternative approach, however, it is worth exploring other options that have been canvassed.

2.3 Thinking of alternatives

One idea is to double down on neoliberalism, on the grounds that it might be – as Churchill said of democracy – the worst model apart from all the others. The notion that a model that has delivered an age of insecurity is the best of a bad bunch is, of course, a far cry from the expansive claims made by the new right in the late 1970s and 1980s, when voters were assured that de-regulation, curbs on unions and privatisation were a necessary and purgative cure for the West's sclerotic economies.

Various other arguments in favour of neoliberalism have been suggested: that the sub-prime mortgage crisis that sparked the crash of 2008 was the result of too much government interference rather than too little; that the tightening of banking regulation and supervision in the wake of the Great Crisis has made the financial system less prone to collapse; and that the new technologies being developed by a new cadre of entrepreneurs will re-invigorate globalised and financialised capitalism. These arguments are variations on a theme: neoliberalism hasn't failed – it just hasn't been properly tried.

The second idea is that the UK suffers from a deficiency of demand and so the answer to its problems lies with looser monetary and fiscal policy. Clearly, getting the demand side of the economy right matters. Interest rates have been kept too high since 2022, presumably to defeat inflation, and the pursuit of arbitrary rules for government borrowing means there is a danger of Britain being caught in an austerity doom loop. That is, low growth leads to pressure to increase taxes and cut expenditure to balance the books, which in turn leads to even slower growth.

To avoid this disastrous development, the Bank of England should be recognised for what it is – a political vehicle – and elected politicians should take back democratic control over interest rates. Similarly, the Office for Budget Responsibility should not effectively be running fiscal policy, especially when it comes to public investment. A competitive exchange rate is also needed to boost exports and reduce the trade deficit. All that said, the lesson from China is that the transformation of Britain will require boosting industry and that requires more than setting interest rates at a level that stimulates growth. It will require more than simply ensuring the exchange rate is at a level that makes manufacturing exports easier to sell abroad, and more even than imposing tariffs. All these factors matter, but they have to operate in the context of a coherent strategy to boost Britain's industrial sector for the modern era.

The reasons are clear. The lesson of the UK's recent past is that, without a solid and thriving productive base, cuts in interest rates boost growth by stimulating consumer spending and the housing market. Britain is a medium-sized country with a tax system that encourages owner-occupation, so the abandonment of controls on capital since the 1970s removed a key mechanism for controlling house prices. As a result, cuts in interest rates have been accompanied by a series of property boom-busts, each of which has further eroded the UK's manufacturing capability.

A lack of industrial capacity has meant the UK has been unable to secure the benefits of a fall in the value of the pound, with a lower level for sterling having a more marked impact on the price of imports than on the volume of exports. Any attempt to rebuild the industrial base of the UK will be stillborn without sufficient demand for domestically produced goods. Getting the demand side of the equation right matters, but the real weakness of the economy lies on the supply side.

A third idea is for progressive parties to smooth some of the rough edges of the pure neoliberal model and come up with a form of compassionate capitalism. Broadly, this was how ruling parties operated in the three decades after the Second World War, which were years of strong growth, full employment and a reduction in inequality. But these goals were only possible because governments could influence the economy through the use of capital controls, state ownership of key sectors, tariffs and control of immigration. Once the main parties bought into the idea that there was no alternative to neoliberalism, governments were faced with the choice of full employment or keeping the financial markets sweet. The latter won out every time.

Tony Blair's 'third way' was an attempt at reconciling obeisance to the market with progressive goals, with the first act of the 1997 Labour government being the decision to grant operational independence to the Bank of England. Gordon Brown, Blair's chancellor, stuck to tough public spending targets inherited from the outgoing Conservative government. Brown called this 'prudence for a purpose' and his approach had some ostensible success in its early years. In the end, however, the third way proved to be smoke and mirrors, with high growth rates largely dependent on cheap imports from China. There was also a Faustian bargain with the City of London in which Labour turned a blind eye to wild speculation in order to cream off some of the proceeds in tax.

Once the financial bubble of the 2000s burst, the tax receipts dried up, the budget deficit ballooned and in 2010 the coalition government of Conservatives and Liberal Democrats imposed austerity measures in an attempt to balance the books. That proved a serious mistake because spending cuts and tax increases slowed economic growth, resulting in borrowing overshooting its targets. It is striking that even while in opposition prior to winning the 2024 election the Labour Party was advocating a somewhat similar approach, cutting back the ambition of its green prosperity plan in order to demonstrate commitment to fiscal rectitude. Meanwhile, the hollowing out of industry continued apace. Britain's output of paper, oil, steel, chemicals and cement – the building blocks for a revival of manufacturing – fell by thirty per cent or more between 2021 and 2024.

Last, but not least, there is the idea that the UK should rejoin the European Union or if that is not possible consider again becoming part of the single market. For those who have never got over the shock of losing the referendum in June 2016, Brexit was a mistake of historic proportions that needs to be reversed. This view ignores some awkward truths, not least that the EU is a failed neoliberal project. With its aim of removing barriers to goods, services, capital and people, the single market was very much a Thatcherite construct. Democratically elected governments were stripped of the power to control their borders, to decide the level of migration, to provide support for growing industries, to change procurement rules to favour domestic businesses and to regulate the flows of hot speculative money in and out of the country.

In the 2020s the EU has clearly emerged as an economic laggard, while enormous social and political tensions developed internally. UK governments can no longer hide behind the excuse that membership of the EU limits their scope for action. They now have the ability to do more than rely on a superficial, consumer-led dash for growth and instead use the powers at their disposal to build an economy with a strong productive sector. The real constraint does not lie in Brussels but in the lopsided structure of Britain's own economy.

3
Britain's lopsided economy

A traveller visiting Shanghai gazes in awe at the enormous skyscrapers of Pudong, the gleaming transportation system, the affluence of the shopping areas. The wealth of the country is evident in the goods, services, buildings and infrastructure available to its people. The labour of Chinese workers has created obvious material abundance. In other countries, wealth also draws on more plentiful resources, such as the oil of the Middle East, the land of the Canadian Prairies, the coal mines of Australia.

The wealth of a country ultimately depends on the size of the labour force, the skills and training of workers, the tools, equipment and technology available to them, the institutional capacity to coordinate inputs and to transport output over great distances. Not least, creation of wealth also depends on the wellbeing of workers – their real wages, quality of natural environment, access to good housing, health and education. Taken together, these factors underpin the productivity of labour, which is what truly drives wealth creation.

It is not difficult to realise when a country has trouble creating wealth. For broad swathes of its people the availability of goods and services is constrained, the quality of its buildings is poor, its infrastructure looks shabby and frayed. The underlying reason is that the productivity of its labour is not rising systematically, or even at all. Much of Western Europe and the USA began to present that image some time ago, but especially since the Great Crisis of 2007–9.

3.1 Diagnosing the British disease

The symptoms of Britain's persistent economic malaise are many: labour productivity is stagnant; investment in equipment, technology and infrastructure is anaemic; the training of workers is not improving; the labour force relies heavily on migrant recruitment because employers substituted hiring from abroad for domestic training once coordinated systems of skill formation were dismantled; and shortages in highly skilled occupations such as doctors and nurses, engineers and IT specialists have also become prominent in recent years.

If there is to be a cure, however, what is needed is not merely to recognise the symptoms but to diagnose the illness. This is precisely what is missing from 'The UK's Modern Industrial Strategy', the Labour government's plan for making good the damage caused by neoliberalism. Its description of the malfunctioning UK economy, especially the lack of productivity growth and the poor investment performance, is broadly accurate. But the real question is: why are private enterprises not investing sufficiently, financial institutions not providing adequate credit, and the skills of the labour force not improving appropriately?

The 'Plan for Change' offers no answers. It merely states that the government has failed to meet the needs of businesses and then suggests that things could get better if eight sectors of the economy were selected and given a range of economic privileges. These eight sectors are very loosely connected to each other. What makes them stand out is simply that the productivity of labour has risen more in them than in other sectors. And so, the main idea of the 'Plan for Change' is that by offering to these eight sectors cheap electricity, tax breaks, and preferential credit they might do even better and somehow push the British economy towards stronger growth.

This is not a strategy for change but a hopeful shot in the dark. It is based on the belief that private businesses are the dynamic factor of growth and would deliver the desired results if only the government facilitated their operations. It is also convinced that the best environment for growth is free trade in commodities and free flows of capital across borders. But these beliefs are groundless.

The reality is that the weakness of the British economy is directly related to the weak performance of its private businesses. This poor performance was already evident in the 1950s and 1960s but has deteriorated further as a result of the neoliberal policies adopted several decades ago: free trade, free movement of capital and – for much of the period – austerity.

An effective strategy to reboot wealth creation in the UK requires analysing the economic forces, institutions and policies that have brought the country to this pass. Once that is done, the strategy should aim to mobilise the available resources to achieve the desired aim of raising the productivity of labour. The role of government is not to facilitate the operations of businesses but to coordinate the national effort for change by transforming the institutions, practices and structures of a deeply dysfunctional economy. For wealth creation to become more vigorous in Britain, it is necessary to change the correlation of social forces by tipping the balance of power in favour of labour.

A word of warning is necessary. Trade unions are rightly concerned whenever the issue of productivity is raised, especially by employers or government. Usually, the underlying intention is that workers should work harder and longer for the same or lower pay. All such talk about raising productivity should be resisted, not only because it pushes workers to do more for less but also because it does not bring positive long-term economic benefits.

If there is to be sustained wealth creation in the UK, the productivity of labour should rise through deep changes in the economy that include improving the wellbeing of workers. It is, therefore, crucial for organised labour to have its own position in this national debate advocating policies that could deal with the problem in an effective way.

3.2 The blight of globalisation and financialisation

Although Britain's industrial problems first began to surface more than a century ago, the neoliberal framework entrenched in the UK since the first Thatcher government is mainly to blame for the current state of the economy. After several decades, it has resulted in a private sector dominated by large industrial and commercial enterprises as well as large banks and investment funds. The UK also has a huge number of small and medium enterprises, but the tone of the economy is set by bigger companies, which shape investment patterns, employment practices, supply chains and pricing across entire sectors. The private sector has failed to deliver dynamic wealth creation. Its poor performance is related to two characteristic tendencies associated with the conduct of big businesses.

The first is globalisation. Large industrial enterprises regularly cross borders to establish productive capacity abroad, and they have gradually established global production chains by spreading their activities across the world and bringing smaller enterprises from other countries into the chains. The bulk of international trade takes place within these chains as the connected enterprises transact with each other.

The second is financialisation. The large globalising enterprises are heavily involved in financial activities, often

Table 3.1 The sectoral composition of the British economy

Sector	1994	2004	2014	2024
Services	69.0	72.6	79.1	80.4
Industry	30.3	26.6	20.0	18.9
Agriculture	0.6	0.7	0.9	0.7

Source: ONS, Gross domestic product (GDP) output approach, Blue Book 2024 data. Rounded to one decimal place.

distributing profits to shareholders and managers instead of reinvesting. At the same time, large banks and investment funds have spread their tentacles throughout the domestic economy and internationally. They extract profits from financial transactions and engage in speculative portfolio activities with stocks and shares, often directly exploiting the income and savings of workers. But they do not systematically support the creation of wealth.

Driven by this private sector, the British economy lacks dynamism, tends to crisis, and is deeply inequitable. Fundamental to its weaknesses is that it has a relatively shrunken industrial sector compared to a greatly enlarged service sector. As Table 3.1 makes clear, the British economy has become overwhelmingly service-based with a comparatively small industrial sector.

Services are not separate from material production but depend heavily on manufactured inputs, including machinery, chemicals, metals, energy systems, transport equipment, data infrastructure. Finance, logistics, healthcare, education, the creative industries all rest on this material base and, without domestic capacity to produce these goods, an economy must import them, which is exactly what Britain does.

The result is a persistent current account deficit that has defined Britain's external position since 1984. This deficit is sustained by continuous capital inflows, which, over time, harden into foreign claims on domestic income and control. Ownership shifts outward; infrastructure and regulated utilities become income streams for foreign-owned operators and global investment funds; property becomes an asset class for sovereign wealth funds and private equity; firms are bought, stripped, and traded. This is not a neutral financial adjustment but a structural condition in which Britain finances consumption and investment by surrendering control over its productive and social assets. The persistent external deficit is the mark of a subordinate economy.

The claim that advanced economies can specialise in high-value services while outsourcing production is false, resting on the illusion that productivity and wages in services can rise independently of what happens in manufacturing. They cannot. When manufacturing declines, service employment tends to be low-productivity, low-wage work. A financial elite emerges extracting vast profits, while the majority are employed in call centres, distribution warehouses, retail, hospitality, and personal services on poverty pay. This is not economic development but the decomposition of a productive into financialised economy backed by mass low-wage labour.

Although the use of artificial intelligence could have a massive impact on the service sector in the coming years, many service sector jobs are labour intensive and unlikely to be replaced by machines. Manufacturing is capital intensive, meaning individual workers have more machinery to work with; it systematically introduces advanced technology in its operations, such as robotics and automation; and it benefits greatly from economies of scale so that as production expands output per worker increases and the cost of manufactured goods comes down. In general, services tend to be labour intensive, rely less on advanced technology, and enjoy fewer economies of scale.

Moreover, manufacturing is deeply connected to other economic activities, both 'upstream' (input) and 'downstream' (output), thus contributing widely to the growth of productivity in other areas of the economy. In contrast, services tend to look 'downstream' and are connected to fewer other activities, thus having a more modest impact on productivity across the economy. Manufacturing is the sector where labour productivity rises most systematically through mechanisation, automation and technical change embedded in capital investment. Material transformation is easier to mechanise than most service activities, and scale economies are more readily achieved. Services include some high-productivity sectors but also vast expanses of retail, hospitality, care work and personal services that resist strong productivity growth. When manufacturing declines, the economy shifts towards these low-productivity service activities while gains tend to concentrate in finance, leaving the majority in stagnant-wage work.

Manufacturing also matters because working-class power has historically been strongest there, meaning productivity gains translate into wage increases rather than being captured as profit. It concentrates workers, creates common conditions, and makes collective action effective, while skills are formed on the job and through apprenticeships tied to production needs. Unions gain leverage because withdrawing labour halts output, and wages are linked to productivity because the threat of strike action is real.

When manufacturing is destroyed, workers do not move into equivalent roles but are scattered into fragmented service sectors with weak bargaining power, high turnover and downward pressure on pay. The collapse of British manufacturing was a class victory for capital that broke union strength, dismantled communities built around production and shifted the balance of power decisively against labour. Regional inequality widened accordingly because production had been geographically concentrated in the Midlands, the North, Scotland and Wales. These regions bore the heaviest costs, while the South East, anchored by finance, took most of the gains.

The historic crisis of 2007–9 marked the peak of both financialisation and globalisation in Britain, exposing the weaknesses in both. The peaking of financialisation and globalisation can be seen in the path of the productivity of labour. Figure 3.1 shows that productivity rose in the early

Figure 3.1 The path of labour productivity

2000s, albeit weakly. After the crisis of 2007–9, however, and even more after the pandemic crisis of 2020–1, productivity remained essentially stagnant. Britain's wealth creation engine stalled.

Moreover, forty years on from the industrial collapse of the 1980s, there are tremendous regional disparities in the productive structure of the UK, among the most severe in Europe. The worst outcomes for productivity growth are to be found in Wales, the North, the Midlands and Scotland. These are areas with historically high urban density and a long history of industrial production. The difference compared to growth in South-East England, including the London region, home of the financial sector, is pronounced, and so is the difference in disposable income among the people of these regions.

There are several reasons for the poor performance of UK labour productivity over a long period of time, but there is also no doubt that it reflects the shift in the economy away from manufacturing and towards services. As Table 3.1 shows, in 2024 industry contributed about nineteen per cent of the value generated in the British economy, and within that manufacturing around eight per cent. Moreover, manufacturing in Britain has historically been concentrated in the regions that are now lagging far behind London and the South East, and which have been the worst hit from its contraction.

Rebuilding productive capacity is a matter of economic revival but also of sovereignty, because an economy that cannot make steel, chemicals, machinery or power equipment cannot decarbonise on its own terms, cannot secure supply of vital goods in a crisis, and cannot adapt production to meet social needs. The Covid pandemic exposed this brutally. Britain could not secure PPE or diagnostics and was forced into emergency dependence on fragile global supply chains, competing on the world market for basic equipment. Even where vaccines were developed and some production took place domestically, critical inputs, manufacturing stages, and delivery capacity lay abroad. The war in Ukraine revealed energy dependence, and climate breakdown will demand deep industrial transformation, none of which is possible without domestic productive capacity under public control. An integral part of this transformation, however, is to tackle the enormous size of the financial sector.

3.3 Commercial banking and shadow banking loom large

In 2024, the Gross Domestic Product of the UK was roughly £3 trillion, and the financial sector contributed close to nine per cent of it. It was geographically spread across the country, with a significant presence in Edinburgh and Leeds, but its heart lay in the City of London. The City is truly international and by any measure it is tremendously overweight relative to the rest of the economy.

Britain has the largest banks in Europe; it is home to an enormous 'shadow banking' system comprising pension funds, investment funds, hedge funds, insurance companies; it possesses the largest Stock Market in Europe, which is also one of the largest in the world; it has a large and growing fintech network of more than 3,000 enterprises; above all, it houses the enormous Eurodollar market, which comprises trillions of dollar deposits held mostly by European banks in London. In December 2024, the outstanding foreign currency deposits owned by non-UK residents stood at nearly £4 trillion.

This dominant financial sector has failed to boost the country's wealth-producing capacity, and is prone to crises, none bigger than that of 2007–9. The speculative operations of globally operating banks in the USA, the UK, and Western Europe – focusing mostly on housing – led to an economic disaster that visited untold hardship on millions. The pandemic crisis of 2020–1 subsequently exposed the further flaws of globalisation.

3.4 The problem with financial services

A revealing insight into the performance of the UK financial sector is given by its productivity, bearing in mind that it employs just over one million workers, around three per cent of the labour force. Productivity is, of course, a difficult concept to apply to the financial sector since finance produces nothing but merely mediates the provision of credit, facilitates the payment of money, and undertakes the assessment of risk among enterprises. But we do know that the financial system systematically introduces advanced technology, including Artificial Intelligence. And so, we would expect that financial services would become steadily cheaper, as normally happens with manufactured goods, such as cars, over time. That would be an indication of more effective use of skilled labour by finance.

While there are no reliable measurements of the cost of financial services in Britain over time, we have data for US finance, and there is good reason to believe that British finance is not different. Remarkably, the cost of financial services in the USA has remained basically constant over the decades, despite the enormous growth of the financial sector and the steady introduction of advanced technology. Despite phenomenal growth and endless talk of 'modernity' emanating from financial circles, there is no evidence that the leading financial systems are providing their services more cheaply to the rest of the economy.

Its own efficiency aside, there is no sound evidence that the UK financial system has significantly contributed to raising labour productivity across the economy, certainly not by meeting the demand of UK businesses for investment funds. There are no firm grounds for thinking that Britain could tackle its productivity problem by further promoting the growth of the financial sector, as the Labour government's 'Plan for Change' claims.

Meanwhile, financial profits have ballooned. Finance has taken advantage of favourable government policies as well as of its own great power in the economy. Financial expropriation has marked the growth of UK finance, drawing huge profits out of other people's money and wealth, including from workers who borrow to buy houses and pay large sums to use bank services.

Financial profits are often paid as salaries and bonuses and exacerbate the UK's income and wealth inequalities, which are already among the worst in Europe. At the same time, the benefits to the economy are hard to detect. The financial sector is an egregious example of the negative impact that the contraction of manufacturing and the resulting warped economy have had on wealth creation in the UK.

3.5 Aggregate investment dries up

These deep structural factors aside, it is easy to identify the more immediate reason why UK productivity grew slowly for several decades and practically stopped growing

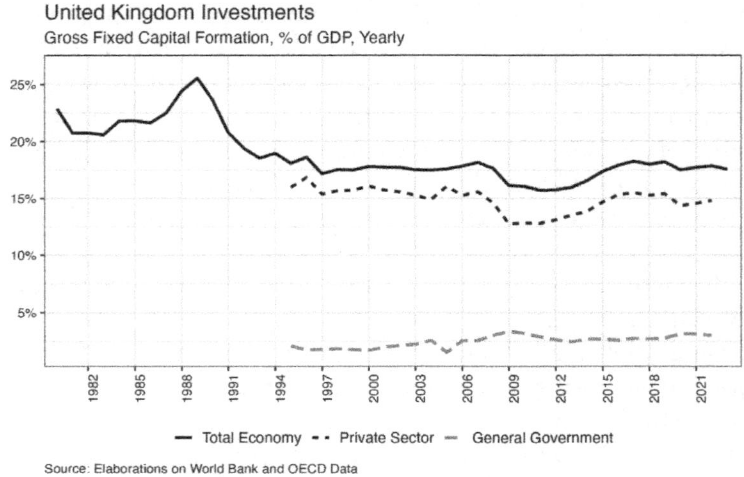

Figure 3.2 The trajectory of investment in the UK aggregate, private and public

after 2007–9. Plainly put, the economy's investment performance has been appalling.

It is clear from Figure 3.2 that Britain has registered low and declining levels of total investment throughout the period of globalisation and financialisation, and the situation worsened notably after the crisis of 2007–9. The culprit is poor investment by both the private and the public sector over several decades.

To understand why investment has been so weak, a look at the UK's net national savings is needed. These savings are the amount left from gross national income after taking out the amount spent on consumption and replenishing the wear and tear of the country's capital stock. They measure the resources available to the country for investment after adjusting for depreciation and indicate whether more capital could be made available to workers, thus potentially raising their productivity.

Figure 3.3 shows the net national savings of the UK as a percentage of its Gross National Income since the early 1990s. Remarkably, the figure has been essentially

Figure 3.3 UK net national savings

Notes: Adjusted savings, net national savings (% of GNI): Net national savings are equal to gross national savings less the value of consumption of fixed capital. This indicator is expressed as a percentage of Gross National Income (GNI) which is the total income earned by all residents within an economic territory during an accounting period. It is equal to gross domestic product plus earned income receivable from abroad minus earned income payable abroad (see: https://databank.worldbank.org/metadataglossary/world-development-indicators/series/NY.ADJ.NNAT.GN.ZS).

negative since the Crisis of 2007–9. For nearly two decades Britain has simply stopped generating a high national income. Even more strikingly, it has given so much weight to consumption that what remains of national income is not enough even to compensate for the depreciation of its capital stock.

Bluntly put, our country has an entirely lopsided economy that places an enormous weight on services – especially finance. To keep this economy going, the country relies on heavy consumption, which is necessary to maintain aggregate demand, but it does not leave enough resources to replenish and expand the available capital. The result is that since 2007–9 Britain has been eating away its accumulated capital stock instead of increasing it. This is the true measure of the failure of both the private and the public sector to invest and generate wealth. No wonder productivity has been stagnating. Truly, British capitalism has been eating itself.

3.6 The private sector fails to invest

Private investment in Britain has been weak for a long time, and key to that is the conduct of big businesses. They hold substantial capital, which they prefer to use to pay dividends to shareholders and high salaries to managers instead of investing for the longer term. Sometimes they use share buybacks, that is, they purchase their own shares from shareholders at inflated prices, but their preferred method is dividend payments.

Following the Crisis of 2007–9, dividend payments and share buy-backs by the largest one hundred UK-domiciled companies escalated enormously. It has been estimated that the total for 2011–18 reached the extraordinary sum of £468 billion.

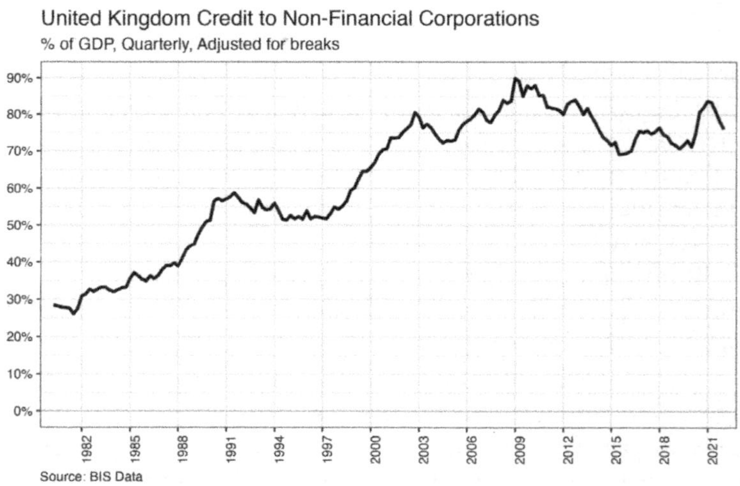

Figure 3.4 UK credit provision to private sector

Notes: Sector lending: All sectors.

Equally important in explaining poor private investment is the weak performance of the financial system, which has consistently provided either too much, or not enough credit to the economy. Figure 3.4 shows the alternation of riches and poverty of credit during the decades of neoliberal domination. The period following the Crisis of 2007–9 was marked by particularly poor credit availability for the economy, matching the poor investment figures.

The lack of credit has been particularly severe for Small and Medium Enterprises (SMEs). It has been estimated that one in ten SMEs is a 'discouraged borrower', that is, an enterprise that does not even approach a bank for credit because it expects to be turned down. If one in ten is a 'discouraged borrower', it is a reasonable conclusion that much larger numbers of SMEs face a permanent shortfall of credit. Even worse, according to the Bank of England, 'discouraged borrowers' are numerous among the more innovative and growth-oriented SMEs.

3.7 And so does the public sector – dominated by the Treasury View

Public investment in the UK has also been persistently weak as is clear from Figure 3.4. Key to that weakness is austerity and the strong ideological commitment of UK governments to the Treasury View. The problem is two-fold. First, the Treasury believes in cutting spending to balance the budget. Second, it tends to cut spending on the things that boost the economy's long-term growth prospects.

Most day-to day public spending is short term and inflexible, such as the wages and salaries of civil servants, drugs for the NHS, or equipment for schools. Consequently, when austerity prevails and the Treasury seeks to cut public expenditure, the first item it will consider is longer-term spending and that means public investment. During the decades of neoliberal austerity, successive UK governments have kept public investment at very low levels, especially after 2007–9. The cumulative impact on UK infrastructure – roads, bridges, transport and affordable public housing – has been ruinous.

Making things even worse is the structure of the British state, which concentrates decision-making power over spending at Westminster. It is a highly centralised system in which ministries – with the Treasury at the top – decide on policy and then expect regional and local implementation. But the mechanisms of local and regional policy delivery in Britain, including in health, transport and education, are diffuse and fragmented.

The sharp contrast between great concentration of state power in Westminster and great fragmentation of state power across the rest of the country has been very problematic for public policy. The process of devolution in Scotland, Wales, and now England, has failed to tackle the problem and perhaps even made it worse, as devolved bodies depend heavily on central government funding. It is perhaps not surprising that public investment, poor as it has been, has favoured the South East and London.

Poor public investment not only keeps aggregate investment low but also negatively impacts on private investment. Strong public investment encourages private investment or, as the economic expression goes, 'crowds in' private investment. When, for instance, rail and roads operate well, they encourage private investment across the country. When they function poorly, as in Britain, they do the opposite, not least by imposing substantial costs on businesses. Stronger private investment requires higher public investment.

Moreover, poor public investment has a negative effect on labour productivity. When commuting is expensive and time consuming, and when the shortage of public housing exacerbates the costs of housing in general, it becomes difficult for workers to move jobs and perform at their best. The lack of public investment over many decades has had an appalling impact on the wellbeing of workers in the UK, affecting their productivity. There can also be little doubt that the great regional disparities of the UK, are directly related to poor public investment and to the power structures of the country concentrating decision-making at Westminster.

In sum, since 2007–9, productivity has flatlined, net national savings have been negative, and both private and public investment have been weak. This stagnant and unbalanced economy has meant chronic trade deficits, reliance on foreign capital, and growing vulnerability to the choices of others.

4
The state we're in

Monty Python's parrot sketch is a comedy classic. For the few who have never seen it, it involves a pet shop owner trying to convince a dissatisfied customer that the bird he has bought is not dead but simply resting. The customer is unconvinced, pointing out that the parrot is only able to stand up because it has been nailed to its perch.

It could be argued that the British state is the equivalent of Norwegian Blue in the parrot sketch: it has, as John Cleese said, 'shuffled off this mortal coil and is pushing up the daisies'. This is not the case, however. The state is not dead. Nor has it been resting for nearly five decades. It has merely been captured by neoliberals. Contemporary capitalism depends on the state absolutely.

To understand why Britain has deindustrialised, it is necessary to examine how the state itself has been reshaped. Deindustrialisation is not simply a sectoral outcome but the result of fiscal, monetary and institutional arrangements that have systematically favoured finance over production. Through these arrangements, large corporations and financial institutions have come to exercise decisive power over the economy. Britain is not exceptional in this respect. Globalised capitalism could not be sustained without active state support for multinational firms and financial institutions. Far from reducing the state's presence in the economy, big business has acquired enormous influence over state economic levers and uses them to serve its own interests. The paradox is that as the state has become more pivotal to the survival of contemporary capitalism its own functioning has become more problematic. The hollowing out of manufacturing has been accompanied by a hollowing out of the state as an agent for change. The state has a remedial function, mopping up the effects of poverty wages, worklessness and ageing, but as a dynamic force it is all but absent.

State capacity is a binding constraint that Britain currently faces and must be addressed. Four decades of outsourcing, cuts and ideological hostility have destroyed technical expertise inside government. Departments lack the staff to design projects, manage contracts, or oversee delivery. Rebuilding capacity requires deliberate action. This includes competitive pay to recruit engineers, project managers and commercial specialists; career structures that reward delivery rather than risk avoidance; in-house teams capable of running complex programmes without dependence on consultants. Partnerships with unions are also essential to draw on sectoral knowledge. All these are vital conditions of sovereignty. A state that cannot deliver what it promises cannot sustain legitimacy or withstand pressure to abandon transformation.

States in several advanced capitalist countries face a near permanent fiscal and monetary crisis because they find it difficult to fund their operations while defending the interests of big business. The crisis is particularly acute in the UK, ultimately because the forces of wealth creation in the country have become deeply disrupted. A national effort to rebuild and transform the British economy must set the restructuring of the British state among its urgent priorities.

4.1 A neoliberal central state that throttles local authorities

The British state is marked by the following characteristics. First, it has a fundamentally antagonistic attitude towards the organisations of the working class, especially the trade unions, aiming to reduce their power and tilt the balance of power in favour of capital. To achieve this aim, the British state has at times mobilised its entire judicial, executive, ideological, and organisational apparatus. The decisive moment was the defeat of the miners in their 1984–5 strike, which marked a long period of retreat for the British working class. Subsequent governments, including the current Labour government, have softened some of the sharpest edges of this settlement, but none has reversed it, and the structural weakening of organised labour has endured.

Second, the state has engaged in sustained privatisation of public property – selling productive assets such as coal and steel, and also housing, transport and utilities. The heaviest episodes were in the 1980s and 1990s, but the preference for keeping the state away from owning and managing productive resources has marked the whole period. The ostensible aims were to raise funds, improve efficiency and widen private ownership.

In all these respects, privatisation proved a failure in the longer term. Funds were raised by selling the nation's 'family silver' but the fiscal predicament of the British state is currently appalling. Efficiency did improve in some industries, such as telecoms and electricity, but that had little to do with private ownership and owed much to regulation and technological advance. And, as for widening private property, the privatisation of large public enterprises through the stock-market, for example in telecoms, did for a short period increase small shareholding but by the 2000s the ownership of shares had become strongly concentrated among big institutions domestically and abroad.

Even in housing, where home ownership increased to a peak of seventy-one per cent by the early 2000s, following privatisation of public housing in the 1980s, the result was to exacerbate the housing crisis by effectively eliminating public investment in housing, forcing millions into rental properties, and encouraging bouts of speculation in house prices.

Third, there is a clear disjuncture between central state and regional/local authorities in Britain. The central state retains enormous power to form economic policy across the country but not necessarily in ways that suit the needs of the regions. Thus, the central state collects more than ninety per cent of the tax revenue, including income tax, national insurance contributions, value added tax, corporation tax, capital gains tax, inheritance tax, and so on.

Local authorities in England, Scotland, Wales and Northern Ireland raise revenue mainly through council tax (on domestic property, based on 1991 valuations) and business rates (on non-domestic properties, such as shops, factories, offices). Even then, council tax increases are capped by the central state, which also largely controls business-rate policy.

Since local authorities are responsible for many public services, which are funded primarily via central government grants, the scope to develop local policy is limited. Moreover, central funding is often short-term, politically driven and subject to cuts when there is a national policy of retrenchment. Borrowing is permitted for capital under the Prudential Code – largely via the Public Works Loan Board – but tighter central controls in recent years, capped increases, and a narrow local tax base (council tax still banded to 1991 valuations) have resulted in chronic under-investment and service degradation in the regions. The centralised character of the British state has meant weaker wealth creation.

Fourth, the British state has managed its finances so that the budget is balanced and borrowing kept to a minimum.

This stance is heavily influenced by the Treasury view that permeates British economic policy-making mechanisms.

A word of caution is important here. Austerity is the knee-jerk response of the British Treasury, but it is not an integral part of neoliberalism, something that happens necessarily because of the condition of the economy, almost like rain in the autumn. It is a policy choice adopted according to circumstances and the British state has abandoned it at critical junctures such as wars but also more recently during the crises of the neoliberal decades.

4.2 Austerity – doing without essentials

Plainly put, austerity amounts to restricting public expenditure, particularly on welfare, while being reluctant to raise taxes, especially on the rich and big business. But the actual mix of expenditure and taxes depends heavily on the condition of the economy at the time. If there is a risk of general crisis, the neoliberal state abandons austerity and spends profusely, as happened during the pandemic of the early 2020s. It is necessary, therefore, to look more closely at both public expenditure and taxation throughout the decades of neoliberalism, shown in Figure 4.1.

The British government reduced public spending as a share of the economy from roughly forty-three per cent of GDP in the early 1980s to under thirty-five per cent by the early 2000s. These were the years of aggressive Thatcherism that dealt a body blow to the British welfare state. The axe fell particularly heavily on spending on public housing and public investment.

This approach was softened by Labour governments in the 2000s, as public expenditure gradually recovered, and austerity was eased. Spending rose to around forty-eight per cent of GDP in the Great Crisis of 2007–9 and was pushed still higher – reaching fifty-three per cent – during the pandemic of 2020–1. Faced with economic meltdown, the neoliberal state rapidly scrapped austerity and boosted spending.

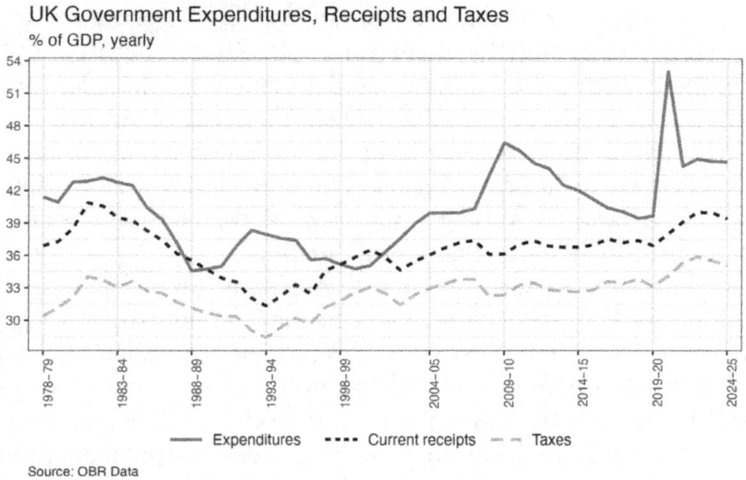

Figure 4.1 Public expenditure (Total Managed Expenditure) and taxation

Notes: 'Public sector current receipts (JW2O), National accounts taxes (GCSU), Total managed expenditure (KX5Q).'

Since the pandemic, public expenditure in Britain has been around forty-five per cent of GDP. This does not mean that all areas of public spending have done equally well. Spending on public housing and on public investment remained considerably lower in 2025 than in the 1970s. Health, on the other hand, fared better, partly because of public support for the NHS. But even here public spending has shifted towards public–private partnerships and the introduction of privatisation in the NHS through the backdoor. The effect on the delivery of health services has been negative.

The only component of public spending that steadily increased since the pandemic is interest on the national debt. Debt-interest outlays were around £100 billion in 2024–5 and about £111.2 billion in 2025–6. This development reflects the crisis confronting the British state and is evidence of the destructive class forces that have risen to the top of British society and warped its economy.

Leaving aside the allocation of public expenditure, it is worth restating the main point: In 2025, the level of public expenditure inherited and pursued by the Labour government was higher than when Thatcher took power. So, when it comes to shrinking the state, neoliberalism has failed even on its own terms. The state is big but in the wrong places, with the growing size of the welfare budget the result of sustained economic torpor.

Moreover, despite constant pressure on Labour to adopt fresh austerity measures for the books to balance, there is no realistic prospect of repeating Thatcher's cuts. The condition of the British economy is so weak that a similar destruction of aggregate demand would ruin the already weakened supply side and cause unprecedented social devastation. If neoliberal capitalism is not to collapse altogether in Britain, the government must continue to engage in substantial public expenditure. This much has been clear since the Great Crisis of 2007–9.

4.3 Taxing times

Turning to taxation, Figure 4.1 shows that the Thatcher years brought a significant reduction, which lasted until the early 1990s. The richest households benefited most, as the rate of income tax was cut from eighty-three per cent to forty per cent for top earners. Big business also benefited as corporation tax was brought down. VAT, which hits the poorest hardest, was increased. This pattern of taxation – favouring the rich and shifting the burden towards indirect taxes – has been a regular feature of the British state.

The steady increase in public expenditure meant that taxes had to increase as proportion of GDP, and so they have never returned to their low point of the early 1990s. The most significant jump took place in the early 2020s aiming to cover some of the fiscal expenditure of the pandemic crisis. The tax intake in the first half of the 2020s rose above the level that Thatcher had inherited in 1979.

Once again, it is obvious that neoliberalism in Britain has failed even on its own terms.

Moreover, since the Great Crisis, the British tax system has become more complex and its burden on the economy heavier. Examples abound: The main rate of VAT rose from 17.5 per cent to twenty per cent in 2011, and has remained at that level; personal tax thresholds were frozen in 2021; National Insurance contributions were raised from 2011 to 2022 and, after declining somewhat, they were again raised in 2025; the main rate of corporation tax, which had gradually been brought down to nineteen per cent after the Great Crisis, was raised to twenty-five per cent in 2023.

Currently, aggregate taxes in Britain are at their highest since the years immediately after the Second World War. Nevertheless, they remain significantly lower than in other major European countries, such as France, Germany and Scandinavia, although they are higher than in the USA. Compared to Europe, furthermore, the UK tax system relies more heavily on indirect taxes, which burden the poor disproportionately. Crucially, the UK taxes wealth more lightly than other European countries. This includes taxation on capital gains, on the value of housing, and on inheritance, which is typically evaded by the rich. British taxes on wealth are low despite the enormous inequality in the distribution of wealth.

After nearly five decades of neoliberalism, Britain has a tax system that favours the wealthy and bears heavily on workers and the poor. As the Public and Commercial Services Union (PCS) has consistently pointed out, simple measures could curb what amounts to tax evasion on a huge scale. The potential revenue is very substantial: charging tax on capital gains at the same rate as on income could raise £12 billion; reinstating the Investment Income Surcharge could yield around £18 billion; introducing an annual wealth tax of two per cent on wealth of more than £10 million could generate at least £22 billion; and abolishing the upper earnings limit on National Insurance would raise £11 billion, according to estimates by His Majesty's Revenue and Customs (HMRC).

Furthermore, real political pressure could be applied to the UK's Overseas Territories and Crown Dependencies to ensure full disclosure of assets held by non-residents, using the UK's own Crown powers if necessary to enforce compliance. Finally, at home, large companies and individuals with incomes above £1 million should be required to make their tax returns public, exposing where taxes are being avoided or evaded.

4.4 Tax and spend and borrow

The combined pressures of expenditure and taxation since the Great Crisis meant that the British government has run persistent fiscal deficits, which require funding mostly through public borrowing in the financial markets. Figure 4.2 provides longer-term evidence on government deficits and shows the change since the Crisis of 2007–9. The

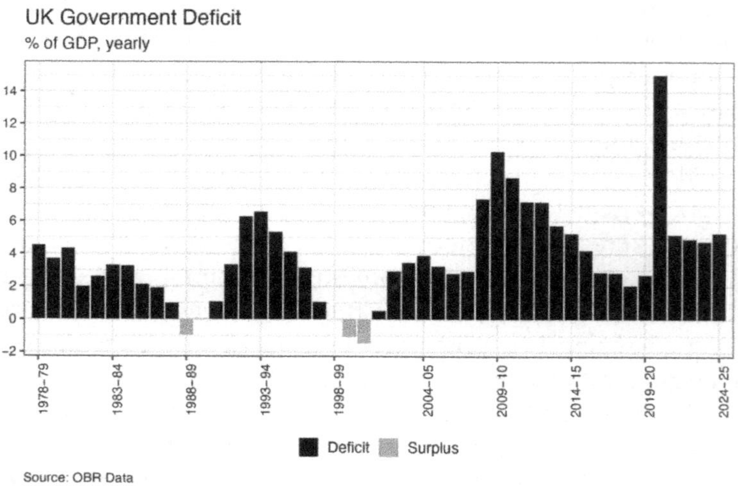

Figure 4.2 The fiscal deficit

Notes: Public sector net borrowing, J5II.

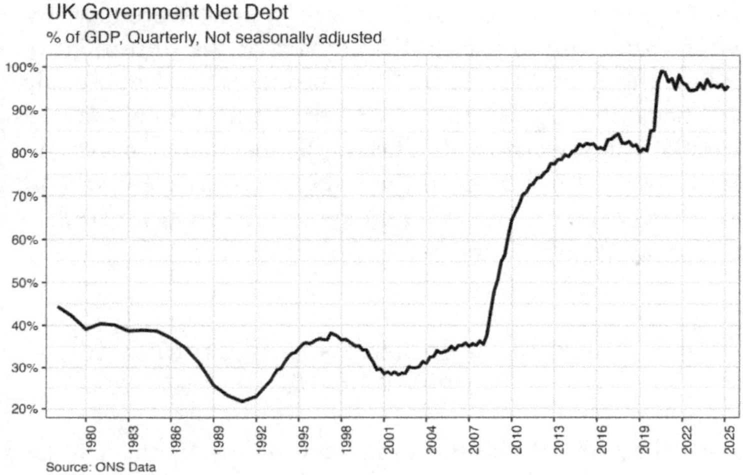

Figure 4.3 Public debt

Notes: PS: Net Debt (excluding public sector banks) as a % of GDP: NSA. Before 1983, only Q1 for each year is recorded.

British state has faced substantial and persistent government deficits.

This is the underlying reality of the fiscal crisis that confronts the Labour government in 2025 and reflects the deep crisis of wealth creation in Britain. A centralised neoliberal state has privatised, outsourced control and deregulated finance; it has to tax heavily because low levels of growth stretching back many years, coupled with a service-sector dominated economy, have been insufficient to fund decent public services.

To finance its persistent fiscal deficits, the British government has sought recourse to the financial markets, and the result has been a sustained increase in public debt. Figure 4.3 shows the jump since 2007–9 to just shy of one hundred per cent of GDP. This is high level for times of peace, exceeded only during the years of the Second World War and the period that immediately followed.

About a third of the debt is held by foreign investors and the rest by domestic lenders. The interest paid on it was not high in the 2010s, since rates of interest were low. But when rates rose in the 2020s as part of the anti-inflation policy, the cost of servicing the debt increased dramatically and became a significant part of the annual fiscal expenditure of the government. The implications are severe and not only on the choices of the Labour government when it comes to deciding on welfare expenditure. They also have a bearing on British monetary policy.

4.5 The Bank of England – public money for private banks

Since the late 1990s, the monetary policy of the UK has been in the hands of an 'independent' Bank of England. The BoE is a public institution and an integral part of the British financial system, especially of the interbank market in which commercial banks and other large financial institutions trade liquidity with each other and determine the market rate of interest.

The BoE's assets are largely public securities, that is, bonds issued by the British government to cover its deficits. Its liabilities are the most fundamental form of money in the country. They are basically banknotes used by households and individuals for small purchases, as well as large deposits that are held by commercial banks and are used to store liquidity or make payments between banks. These liabilities of the central bank are effectively guaranteed by the state and consequently function as the foundational money of the country.

The BoE is always present in the interbank market to make sure that commercial banks have sufficient liquidity to underpin their profit-making operations. If liquidity is short, the BoE will buy securities or lend to banks against collateral. When it provides liquidity, it simply augments the deposits that commercial banks hold at the BoE. This is the meaning of 'money creation' by the central bank in contemporary capitalism. When commercial banks acquire bigger deposits with the BoE, they can expand their own commercial lending and so increase the total amount of private bank deposits in the country. This is how credit money – by far the dominant form of money in Britain – is created.

Bonds issued by the state are the benchmark securities for the central bank, the commercial banks, and other large financial institutions. Moreover, the BoE rate of interest is the reference point for all commercial interest rates. In other words, the deregulated financial markets rely completely on a state institution that trades primarily in state securities and issues state-backed money that then acts as the foundation for the credit money of the country.

Monetary policy basically means managing the volume of liquidity in the financial markets and its price, which is the rate of interest. In contrast to fiscal policy, it appears to be technical and complex, while often operating tacitly. And yet, it has a deeply entrenched class character, even if it is difficult to detect. The central bank supports and subsidises large financial institutions using public credit and public funds.

The meaning of central bank 'independence' is clear in this light. The BoE is the pivotal public institution ensuring that the financial system continues to function and financial institutions make profits. Its operations are 'independent' of parliamentary, or other, electoral processes that normally have a major influence on fiscal policy (especially on taxation) in democratic countries.

In effect, the central bank was made unaccountable within the normal democratic processes of Britain. It has been turned into a realm of technical experts who 'know' how to manage the monetary affairs of the nation. In practice, the BoE has been given enormous powers to serve the interests of the financial system, while transgressing the bounds of democracy.

The role of the 'independent' BoE in confronting the long-term crisis that has slowly emerged after 2007–9 is historically unprecedented. Monetary policy took entirely new dimensions as the central bank adopted Quantitative Easing and brought the rate of interest close to zero for long periods of time. The way in which the BoE achieved this aim was by purchasing huge volumes of the very public debt that the British state issued to fund its persistently high fiscal expenditure.

4.6 The merry-go-round of money

Quantitative Easing was adopted in the 2010s in response to the threat of a second Great Depression generated by the Great Crisis. The BoE acquired nearly a third of British public debt at the peak of Quantitative Easing and paid for it by creating new state-backed money as is shown in Figure 4.4. This merry-go-round was also a mechanism for supporting and subsidising banks and other financial institutions. Commercial banks were able to obtain liquidity very cheaply and subsequently kept it in their deposits at the Bank of England, thus earning risk-free interest. In effect, the state provided a publicly funded subsidy to the financial sector.

The Bank of England obtained securities through its Asset Purchase Facility (APF), which is legally a subsidiary of the BoE and enjoys a full indemnity of any possible losses from the Treasury. In practical terms, the APF receives a loan from the BoE, buys the securities, and earns interest on them. It then pays back the BoE for the loan it initially received. Any surplus income is transferred to the Treasury, and any losses are covered by the Treasury out of public funds.

Quantitative Easing came to an end in 2022 as inflation accelerated. The BoE adopted Quantitative Tightening, stopped expanding its balance sheet and began to contract it, as is also shown in Figure 4.4. It also steadily raised the rate of interest: from 0.10 per cent in March 2020, the rate went to 5.25 per cent in August 2023, the highest since the crisis of 2007–9. But the BoE continues to hold very

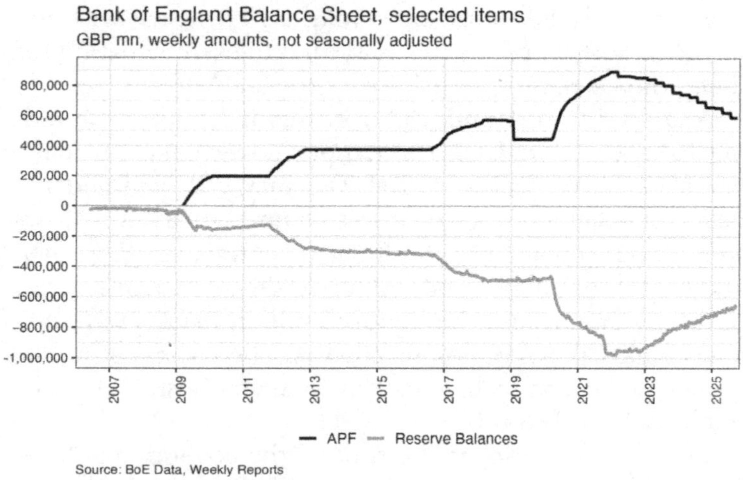

Figure 4.4 The balance sheet of the BoE

Notes: Weekly Reporting (https://www.bankofengland.co.uk/weekly-report/balance-sheet-and-weekly-report) were used instead of the Balance Sheet Data as the latter is only available since 2013. APF ('Weekly amounts outstanding of Central Bank sterling loan to Asset Purchase Facility total (in sterling millions) not seasonally adjusted RPWZ4TM') are only available since September 2013. As an estimate of APF before September 2013 'Weekly stock of holdings of gilts by the Bank of England's asset purchase facility (in sterling millions) YWWB9T9' were used.

large amounts of public securities, which correspond to deposits held by commercial banks at the BoE. The reason is that commercial banks remain deeply worried about the profound instability of the financial system and the British economy and choose to hold huge deposits with the BoE. But the commercial banks are also making secure profits by keeping large BoE deposits.

The BoE pays them the market rate of interest, which, although it declined to 4.25 and then to 3.75 per cent in 2025, remains substantially above the (roughly) 1.5 per cent paid to the government bonds that the BoE holds on its own balance sheet. The BoE makes losses that are effectively a subsidy to commercial banks. Moreover, and astonishingly, the BoE decided that as part of Quantitative Tightening it would contract its assets rapidly by selling government bonds in the open market. The result was that the price of these gilts fell below what the BoE had paid for them, thus generating fresh losses for the APF.

And so, in 2024 and 2025, in the midst of an unfolding fiscal crisis that led the Labour government to make harsh austerity decisions, the Treasury compensated the Bank of England for its losses. Cumulative APF flows were about (plus) £123.8 billion to September 2022, then about (minus) £36.3 billion in 2024–25. Debt-interest outlays were around the hundred-billion mark in 2024–5 and about £111.2 billion in 2025–6. Huge sums of public money were channelled to the financial system via the public debt of Britain.

The class interests at the root of the economic policies adopted by the British state have rarely been more blatant. Meanwhile, the British economy continued to deteriorate, and the livelihood of the British people continued to worsen.

5

Britain's external dependence

5.1 Lopsided economy, unbalanced trade

There was a time, not so long ago, when a poor set of monthly trade figures could lead to a change in government policy. A widening deficit made headlines, with the failure of exports to match imports reported on the TV in the sombre tones of a doctor imparting bad news to a patient. A poor set of trade figures in the week of the 1970 election is supposed to have contributed to Labour's defeat. Over the years interest in Britain's dealings with the wider world has waned, but the fundamental problem has not gone away. Indeed, de-industrialisation has made matters far worse.

Put simply, we sell too few goods and buy too many, and the services we export don't make up the gap. We plug the hole with short-term money from abroad and by selling more of our assets and debt to overseas owners. This means that Britain's standard of living increasingly depends not on what it produces, but on the willingness of foreign investors to keep financing its deficits. That is what external dependence looks like.

This weakness is immediately apparent in the UK's Current Account, shown in Figure 5.1.

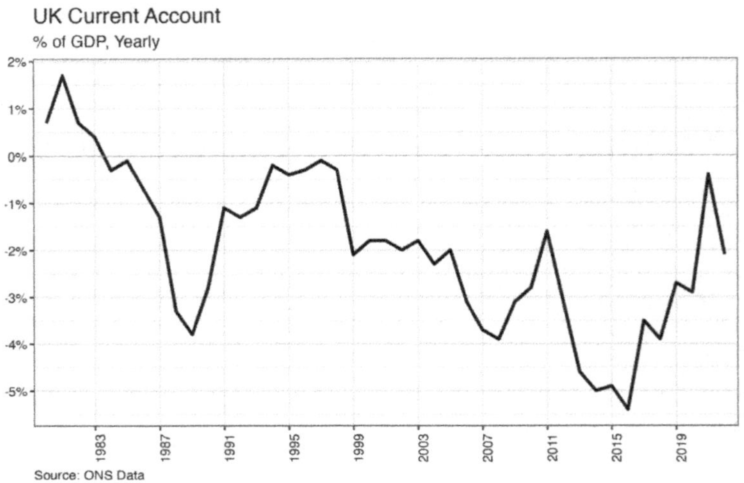

Figure 5.1 UK current account

The Current Account is a gauge of a country's transactions with the rest of the world and has two main components. The first is the Balance of Trade, which records the difference between the country's exports and imports of both goods and services. The second is Net Primary Income, which records the difference between, on one side, the flows of salaries, dividends, interest, and other income coming into the UK from investments and employment of British people abroad and, on the other, the same flows paid out to foreigners for their own investments, employment, and so on in the UK. A persistent deficit of this kind is not a bookkeeping curiosity but a sign that the economy is failing to generate enough value to sustain itself.

The weakness of the UK Balance of Trade since the mid-1980s reflects the shift of the economy away from manufacturing and towards services. In the early 1980s, close to seventy per cent of UK exports were manufactured goods, with services making roughly twenty-five per cent; imports had a similar composition in favour of goods relative to services. By the early 2020s the composition of UK trade with the rest of the world was greatly altered: broadly, exports comprised manufactured goods at thirty-five per cent and services at sixty-five per cent, while imports comprised goods at sixty-five per cent and services at thirty-five per cent.

The reversal in the composition of British exports and imports led to a persistent trade deficit, with a deficit in goods persistently higher than the surplus in services. There is no prospect of this weakness being corrected in the foreseeable future, unless there is a profound change in the structure of the British economy. The service sector is far less export-oriented than manufacturing and it is highly unlikely that the surplus in financial and other services would ever make up the shortfall in the UK's goods trade. Indeed, it is remarkable that manufacturing, which currently stands at less than ten per cent of GDP, continues to contribute more than thirty per cent of the UK's exports. This stark mismatch exposes the fragility of an economic model that sidelines manufacturing while relying on it to earn foreign income.

Making things worse, Britain's stagnant productivity has contributed to its poor trading performance. To be sure, global competitiveness has several determinants, including the availability of natural resources, the means of transport, and the institutional mechanisms that facilitate trading. But the productivity of a country's labour relative to the real wages paid to its workers is the most powerful determinant of a country's trading in goods and services.

5.2 Volatility, fragility and dependence

When a country runs a persistent current account deficit it must attract capital from the rest of the world to balance the books. Britain has not run a manufacturing trade surplus for more than four decades and thus relies systematically on inward capital flows. In effect, the country must continuously persuade global financial investors to cover the gap left by its weakened productive base.

Since neoliberalism dominates economic thinking and policy making, the country has abolished almost all controls on the movement of such capital, which comes in three forms: portfolio flows, banking flows and foreign direct investment flows – all of which are components of the UK's Financial Account with the rest of the world.

Portfolio flows measure the money capital going out from and coming into the UK from trading financial assets (basically shares and bonds). On the one hand, UK financial institutions such as banks and investment funds buy financial assets abroad and, on the other, foreign financial institutions buy UK financial assets.

Banking flows measure the money capital going out from and coming into the UK as banks make loans. UK banks make loans to foreigners, while foreign banks make loans to UK residents.

Foreign Direct Investment (FDI) flows, finally, measure money capital going out from and coming into the UK as enterprises are bought and sold and as new productive capacity is created.

The persistent shortfall in the UK's Current Account has been made good over the decades by net inflows of money capital from abroad on its Financial Account. These net inflows typically occur through portfolio and banking flows, which together bring in more money capital than leaves the country. In 2023, for instance, the UK had a Current Account deficit of £53 billion, roughly two per cent of its GDP. During the same year, total financial inflows were £325 billion and total financial outflows £277 billion, that is a net inflow of roughly £50 billion that effectively balanced the deficit on Current Account.

It might seem, then, that the UK has solved the problem of its persistent deficit on Current Account, but this is not so. Portfolio flows into the UK are volatile, reflecting shifts in global market sentiment, interest rate differentials, and exchange rate fluctuations. They are notoriously speculative and depend on changes in monetary policy in the core countries of the world economy, especially in the USA, which crucially affect global interest rates and exchange rates. Portfolio flows also depend on major geopolitical developments, such as the Brexit referendum in 2016, following which portfolio managers took equity funds out of the UK.

What holds for portfolio flows also effectively holds for banking flows in and out of the UK. They are volatile and often speculative as banks seek funding for their activities across the world. The potential sources of such funding for banks – and hence their own lending – constantly change as banking regulations are altered across borders, and the monetary policy of various governments shifts, thereby changing interest rates and exchange rates.

Finally, FDI is also highly volatile and in practice different from the popular image of foreign enterprises coming to the UK to establish new productive capacity. The majority of FDI flows into the UK are not in new car plants or AI data centres but result from cross-border mergers and acquisitions, that is, from the acquisition of existing UK enterprises by foreign firms. In contrast, 'greenfield investment', i.e., new productive projects or expansions of existing projects, represents a much smaller share of total inflows. Inward FDI flows peaked in 2016 at £192b, but that very high figure was distorted by the £79 billion takeover of brewer SABMiller and the £24 billion takeover of chipmaker ARM.

Moreover, the bulk of inward FDI goes to financial services, professional services, and real estate, rather than to productive activities. In short, inward FDI mirrors the warped structure of the British economy. The recipients are often banks, insurance companies, and portfolio managers, and the money capital coming in mostly reflects balance sheet movements, such as capital injections and regulatory capital reallocation. Real estate is a favourite sector for inward FDI, with money capital sent by global speculators seeking rents and capital gains through property appreciation. What appears as foreign 'investment' is therefore often a transfer of ownership rather than an expansion of productive capacity.

This method of balancing the books has created real problems for Britain. To tackle its persistent deficit on goods and services, the country relies on the volatile and speculative choices of the owners and the managers of money capital, which moreover crosses borders without controls. Consequently, the UK must adjust its fiscal and monetary policies according to the preferences and concerns of these people, ensuring that its interest rates and the exchange rate of the pound are such that they can continue to make profits. At the same time, large profits are also made by firms based in the City of London that actively participate in the flows of capital.

And so, a great axis of power has emerged during the decades of neoliberalism between the state mechanisms advocating the 'Treasury View', the financialised enterprises that operate globally, and the various institutions of the City of London. They seek to maintain these international arrangements, and exercise enormous influence on the British government to pursue fiscal and monetary policies that are compatible with them. The costs for the rest of the economy are substantial, not least as the financial speculators are strong supporters of fiscal conservatism and austerity.

Box 5.1 Foreign Ownership and the Loss of Economic Control

Britain's persistent current account deficits have been financed partly by borrowing and partly by selling off ownership of assets and income streams. Over time, this has left large parts of the economy under foreign control, while increasing the country's external debt. By 2022, foreign investors owned 57.7 per cent of UK quoted company equity by value, one of the highest shares among major advanced economies. Foreign ownership is especially concentrated in infrastructure, utilities, property and key service sectors. Manufacturing has also been hollowed out through overseas takeovers, leaving few strategic sectors under domestic control.

Strategic assets illustrate the pattern clearly. Most major UK airports are majority-owned by overseas investors: Heathrow by Qatar, China and Singapore; Gatwick by VINCI (France); Manchester Airport Group by IFM Investors (Australian superannuation funds). Foreign pension funds and sovereign wealth funds treat UK airports as income-generating assets rather than as key elements to improve the country's productive capacity.

All water companies in England are foreign owned, typically via complex corporate structures involving private equity and offshore holding companies. As an example, Thames Water, serving fifteen million people, is owned by a consortium, including the Ontario Municipal Employees Retirement System (Canada), the Abu Dhabi Investment Authority, and China Investment Corporation, structured through offshore intermediaries in the Cayman Islands.

Large parts of the UK energy system are controlled from abroad. Electricity generation and networks are dominated by foreign-owned companies, including state-owned utilities from France and Scandinavia and infrastructure groups based in the United States and East Asia. Électricité de France (EDF Energy), owned by the French state, operates all UK nuclear power stations and remains the largest electricity generator. Electricity distribution networks are owned largely by overseas investors, including foreign pension funds and infrastructure conglomerates. Offshore wind, central to meeting Net Zero targets, is dominated by non-UK developers, with investment decisions, supply chains and profits largely determined outside Britain. In these sectors, revenues generated from British households and firms are routinely distributed abroad rather than reinvested domestically.

Rail provides a particularly clear example of how foreign ownership and financialisation have operated in practice. Following privatisation, the British rail system was reorganised so that core assets and revenue streams were separated from operational responsibility. Rolling stock is owned by private leasing companies and supplied predominantly by foreign multinationals, including Siemens, Hitachi, Alstom and CAF. Domestic manufacturing capacity has been marginalised, while procurement decisions are shaped by global corporate strategies rather than national industrial needs. At the same time, Network Rail has accumulated a large stock of private debt, much of it index-linked and effectively guaranteed by the state. By the mid-2020s, this debt exceeded £50 billion, and rising interest rates sharply increased annual financing costs, diverting resources away from maintenance, investment and service improvement. The state absorbed risk, while returns accrued to private creditors and suppliers, many of them overseas.

This pattern is not confined to rail. Across the economy, inward foreign direct investment has been dominated by mergers and acquisitions rather than greenfield investment. Ownership changes hands, but productive capacity does not expand. The income consequences are visible in the UK's external accounts, where net primary income has increasingly turned negative as payments to foreign owners exceed income earned abroad.

Foreign ownership is not incidental to Britain's external dependence but constitutive of it. Persistent trade deficits have been financed by selling productive assets, infrastructure and future income streams, shifting control over investment decisions, pricing, and long-term industrial strategy overseas.

Reindustrialisation cannot succeed while strategic decisions remain in foreign boardrooms optimising returns for overseas shareholders. Energy security is impossible when generation, networks and fuel supply are foreign-controlled. Productivity growth stalls when procurement feeds global supply chains rather than domestic capacity.

The industrial strategy developed in Chapters 8–11 addresses this directly, setting out how public ownership, procurement policy, and controls on capital flows can be used to reverse outward transfers of ownership and anchor productive capacity and income within Britain.

5.3 Between a rock and a hard place

Relying on the free flows of money capital constrains the government of Britain and offers no clear advantages to its economy. But it is even worse than that in the long term. For, the net inflow of money capital through the Financial Account is largely a debt owed to foreigners who have bought British financial assets or made bank loans to British residents. It is also money capital coming to buy the infrastructure and the productive resources of the country.

If Britain systematically relies on such net inflows, it follows that it is accumulating more debt (liabilities) to foreigners than the debts (liabilities) of foreigners to British residents. It is becoming steadily more indebted abroad and must ensure that it is able to pay to foreigners what it owes them annually, including interest. It must also ensure that foreigners are ready and willing to absorb the fresh volumes of debt that Britain seeks to obtain from them annually. Over time, this shifts power outward, as policy must increasingly be shaped to reassure creditors rather than to meet domestic needs.

A useful measure of Britain's dependence in this respect is given by its Net International Investment Position, which basically sums up the liabilities owed by British residents abroad compared to liabilities of foreigners owed to Britain. It is far from an accident that the UK's Net International Investment Position for most of the period since 2007–9 has been strongly negative. The stalling of the engine of wealth creation has led to a further weakening of the country's international position and turned it into a major international borrower.

The dependence of the UK on foreign lenders, finally, is also shown by the extent to which foreigners hold UK government debt. The proportion has increased substantially since 2007–9 and currently stands between thirty and forty per cent. Consequently, the ability of the British government to borrow and thus implement the fiscal policies for which it was elected depends on the speculative decisions of foreign lenders. The current Labour government has already discovered the political cost of such dependence.

The current predicament of Britain is far more serious than would appear by simply noting the stagnant productivity of labour. When wealth creation stalls in a capitalist economy, the problem soon stretches to society, politics, and international affairs. Britain urgently needs a drastic change of direction away from neoliberalism. It requires a strategy that will transform its lopsided economy, restart wealth creation, and alter the social balance in favour of labour.

Taken together, Britain's lopsided economy at home and its dependence abroad mark a structural impasse. External dependence reinforces internal weakness, locking Britain into low growth, high inequality, and constrained policy choices. The country cannot rely on private enterprise, finance, or foreign inflows to restart wealth creation. A different path, led by public initiative and grounded in labour, is the only way forward.

6
Hard labour

6.1 Gross inequality

Downton Abbey is one of the great export successes of Britain's creative industries. Set in the period before, during and after the First World War, it tells the story of life in an English country house, with as much attention paid to the servants living downstairs as to the Earl of Grantham and his family above stairs. The gulf between the classes is vividly portrayed.

Written by the Conservative peer Julian Fellowes, *Downton Abbey* is supposed to be a nostalgic trip down memory lane to a romanticised world that is no more. Yet, while the days of under-butlers are no more, the current levels of inequality mean the Britain of 2026 bears more than a passing resemblance to that of a century ago. Income inequality has been rising since the 1980s and Britain is one of most unequal countries in Europe. The long-promised trickle down never materialised.

The rise of inequality is shown in Figure 6.1. The richest ten per cent of the population receives thirty-five per cent of Britain's income after decades of seeing its share rise, especially in the 1980s, 1990s and 2000s. Meanwhile, the

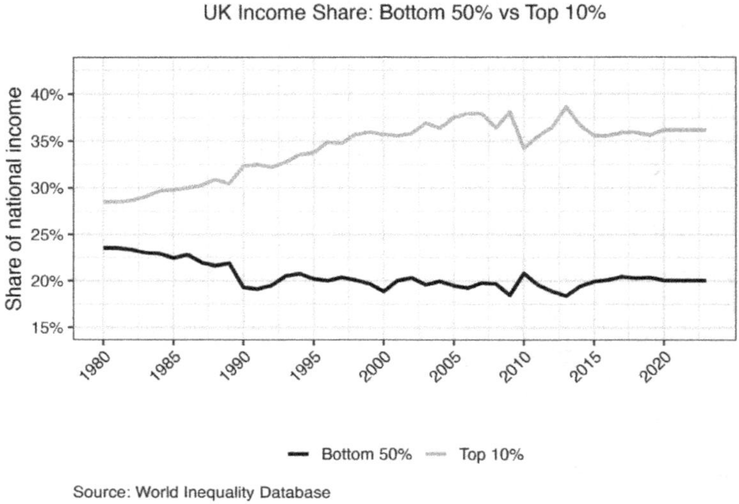

Figure 6.1 Income inequality, top 10%, bottom 50%

bottom fifty per cent has witnessed the decline of its own share, especially in the 1980s, and currently receives about twenty per cent of the total.

But the true magnitude of income inequality becomes clear only when we consider the top one per cent compared to the bottom fifty per cent of the UK population in Figure 6.2.

The top one per cent saw its share rise greatly in the 1990s and 2000s and currently receives 13.1 per cent of the total income. There is no doubt that the distribution of income in the UK has become heavily skewed in favour of the very rich in the years of neoliberal ascendancy. The contrast with the twenty per cent received by the bottom fifty per cent of the population is obscene.

Bad as the inequality of income has become, the condition of labour in the UK is shown in a far more dramatic light when the distribution of wealth is also taken into consideration in Figure 6.3.

Figure 6.3 shows that the share of the richest one per cent of the population in the nation's wealth declined in

Figure 6.2 Income inequality, top 1%, bottom 50%

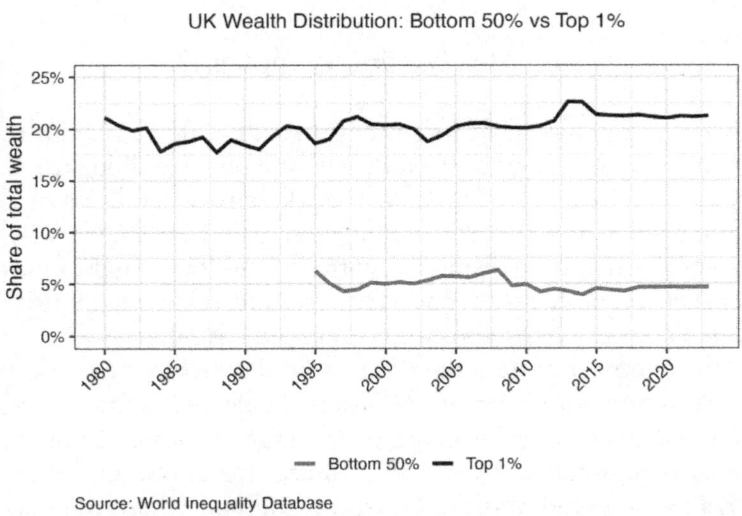

Figure 6.3 Wealth inequality, top 1%, bottom 50%

the early 1980s but has been on a steady upward trend since then. Currently, the richest one per cent holds more than twenty per cent of the country's total wealth. During the same period, the share of the bottom fifty per cent of the population hovered around five per cent of the total. The proportion even declined slightly after the Great Crisis of 2007–9 and fell below five per cent. That was exactly at the same time as the share of the top one per cent increased further.

Britain is one of the most unequal countries in the world, with extreme wealth differences between the richest one per cent and the bulk of the population. The profound transformation of the labour force and the worsening of inequality since the 1980s are inextricably linked to the weakening of labour, the retreat of its independent presence in national affairs, and the loss of its voice in public debates. Labour has been immeasurably weakened in the UK during the years of neoliberalism, and its weakness is visible in the destruction of traditional communities and the demise of workers' cultural institutions.

6.2 Flexible and compliant?

Britain now has what its supporters call a 'flexible' labour market: a weasel word if ever there was one. Flexible means your employer can make you work harder while paying you a wage that makes it a struggle to pay the bills. Flexible means you can be dismissed without a union to fight your corner. Flexible means the cards are stacked against workers. Flexible means you can be exploited grossly.

The impact of de-industrialisation on the labour market was swift and enduring. Workers made redundant were parked on sickness benefits to massage the official unemployment figures. Even today there are communities in Wales, Scotland and the North of England where the real jobless rate is much higher than the official rate. Well-paid unionised jobs in factories were replaced by insecure, non-unionised jobs in call centres and distribution warehouses. Many of the jobs went to workers from overseas. The abiding features of the flexible labour market are insecurity, casualisation, low productivity and poor pay.

Britain's employers vigorously oppose any attempts to shift the pendulum back in favour of workers. They lobbied hard for the current Labour government to soften the terms of its already modest employment rights legislation and warned that any tightening of immigration controls would jeopardise the business models of sectors such as higher education, agriculture and hospitality. All of which begs the question of whether these business models are viable at all if they depend on an unlimited supply of cheap labour. There are better solutions, but they involve breaking with the neoliberal flexible labour market.

6.3 Reshaping labour

Here's an alternative take on where Britain's labour force stands today. Table 6.1 shows that, in 2025, more people were employed than ever before – 34 million – out of a total population that had also increased substantially – 69 million.

The labour force is very different to fifty years ago, reflecting both the transformation and the underlying weaknesses of UK capitalism during that period. Of the 34 million workers in the current labour force, eighty-five per cent work in the service sector, and only thirteen per cent in industry. The number of part-time workers has doubled, from around four million in the 1970s to 8.5 million in 2024. Moreover, the actual working age has increased in

Table 6.1 British population and labour force

Decade	Population (mn)	Working-age population (mn)	Labour force (mn)
1990s	57	34	28
2000s	60	36	29
2010s	65	42	32
2024	69	43	34

Source: ONS, various. Rounded to nearest integer. The figure of the labour force refers to ages 16–64 (excludes 65+).

practice, and at least two million people over 65 are in active employment, in addition to the 34 million of regular working age. Women now make up a far larger proportion of the workforce, rising from thirty-nine per cent in the 1970s to forty-eight per cent in 2024, and are far likelier than men to work part-time – thirty-six per cent of women compared to fourteen per cent of men in 2024. At the same time, more people are economically inactive – nine million out of a working age population of 43 million – often citing ill-health as the reason. Inactivity was particularly notable among young people after the pandemic, and it affected more heavily several de-industrialised areas of the country. Finally, the number of workers who were born overseas has increased substantially – the proportion rose from about four per cent in the late 1990s to close to fifteen per cent in 2024.

6.4 Pressing down real wages

When labour productivity fails to rise systematically, the ability of enterprises to compete in the markets and extract profits is severely constrained. Capitalism is predicated on businesses making profits by producing more cheaply than their rivals, and the surest way for an enterprise to succeed in price competition is to raise the productivity of labour. When sustained productivity increases are not available, enterprises must find other ways to succeed, and the most obvious option is to keep real wages down.

Applying downward pressure on real wages has been the preferred method of profit extraction by British employers for a long time, and certainly since the Crisis of 2007–9, as Figure 6.4 shows.

The years following the pandemic crisis of 2020–1 have been very harsh, as price inflation accelerated, and productivity growth stalled. Real wages suffered and the disposable income of workers fell, giving rise to a cost-of-living crisis. Millions experienced unprecedented poverty and that was

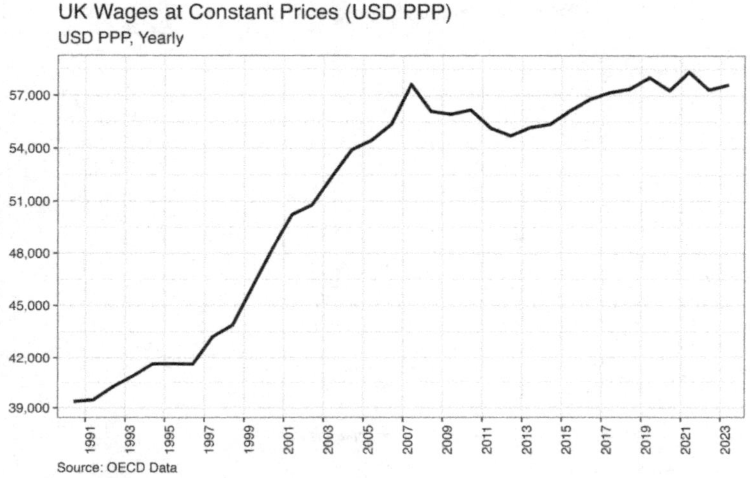

Figure 6.4 UK real wages

after more than a decade of persistent downward pressure on their incomes. Even when workers had regular jobs, hundreds of thousands were unable to meet basic food needs. During the same period, big businesses made enormous profits, using their market power to force prices up.

A key reason why British employers have been able for a long time to press real wages downwards is because trade unions have been weak, especially in the private sector. Employers have also relied on legislation that has consistently supported capital against labour; finally, since the late 1990s, they have taken advantage of large-scale inflows of migrant workers.

Figure 6.5 shows that net migration in Britain in the 2000s and 2010s was driven primarily by workers from the EU, that is, mostly workers from Eastern Europe; by mid-2020s they comprised sixty per cent of immigrant workers. After the Brexit referendum of 2016, immigration from the EU turned negative as European workers left Britain. At the same time, immigration by non-EU workers began to increase and by the mid-2020s they were fifty-five to sixty per cent of the total number of immigrant workers.

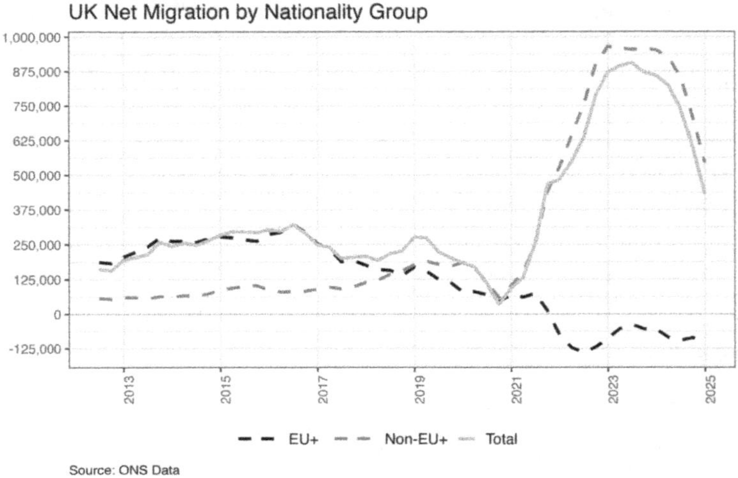

Figure 6.5 UK net migration

The most striking aspect of Figure 6.5, however, is the extraordinary escalation of net migration in the early 2020s. Much of the increase was due to overseas students enrolling in higher education and to dependants arriving to join family members living in Britain. According to the Office for National Statistics, the number of people coming to the UK to study almost tripled from 119,000 in the year to June 2019 to 302,000 four years later. Young people from overseas filled gaping holes in UK universities' finances, and the recruitment of students became a lucrative private business. Faced with the reality of punishing living costs in the UK, many of these students ended up in financial distress and in the informal labour market. The same release showed the continuing impact of Britain's colonial past on flows, with India providing more migrants to the UK in 2024 – 58,000 – than any other country. Nigeria – with 15,000 migrants – was third on the list.

High levels of immigration by workers recruited into low-wage sectors has long been a systematic practice of the British establishment to maintain profitability by exploiting those who usually lack trade union organisation and do not have supporting networks of family and community. The peak was reached in 2023 and although numbers began to fall after that, the influx remained substantial.

This policy allowed British employers to avoid the productive investment needed to transform the economy. The result was abundant labour alongside chronically low productivity, as employment shifted further towards low-wage service work instead of industry. Breaking this pattern requires raising the proportion of workers in industry while drastically reducing the proportion in poorly paid, insecure service jobs. The contribution that immigration can make to this change of direction is discussed in the following chapters.

6.5 Back to work

Finally, the failure of wealth creation in the UK together with the shift towards low-productivity services and bad jobs as well as the deep insecurity and uncertainty about the future have had a significant impact on the readiness of young people to join the labour force. As was already mentioned in the previous sections, economic inactivity has increased rapidly among the young since the pandemic. This is a very negative development for the prospects of rebuilding the British economy.

Things look even worse when the regional allocation of inactivity rates is taken into consideration, as is shown in Table 6.2.

The proportion of economically inactive workers is considerably higher in the regions of Britain that have had the most pronounced loss of industrial employment and continue to have the greatest difficulty in adjusting to the new, globalised and financialised, economy that focuses on services. The destruction of workers' jobs and communities in the historic industrial centres of the country has resulted in local economies with lower productivity and poor-quality jobs. This has contributed to the higher

Table 6.2 Regional rates of economic inactivity in the UK, August 2025

North East	28.2
North West	22.8
Yorkshire and the Humber	23.9
East Midlands	21.2
West Midlands	21.9
East	17.5
London	20.1
South East	17.7
South West	17.0
Wales	24.8
Scotland	21.9
Northern Ireland	26.6

Source: Labour Force Survey, ONS

inactivity proportions among working-age people in those regions.

The UK labour force currently reflects both the transformation and the underlying weaknesses of UK capitalism. The labour force grew considerably as the population expanded, and much of its growth was due to the entry of women and immigrants. However, it is heavily skewed towards services in line with the decline in manufacturing and thus reflects the generally lower productivity of the service sector. A significant part of the labour force is taken up by part-time and other casual workers, and that part is dominated by women. Economic inactivity and even unwillingness to join the labour force, finally, have become more pronounced among young people, especially in the regions of the UK that have lost industrial capacity.

The UK has great reserves of labour power available to it but if it is to rebuild its economy aiming to raise the productivity of labour and create wealth, it will need to alter the composition and the outlook of its labour force. Above all, the country needs to raise the proportion of workers in industry, while drastically reducing the proportion in poorly paid and insecure jobs of low productivity that are typically associated with services.

The reindustrialisation programme that we advocate in this book is based on internationalism and recognises that British-born and migrant workers share the same class position under capital, facing employers who seek to extract maximum value at minimum cost. When employers can recruit workers denied union rights, pay them below domestic norms, and house them in overcrowded conditions while British-born workers face unemployment or casualised contracts, capital divides the working class along lines of origin and legal status.

Workers from Poland or Pakistan have no inherent interest in undercutting wages any more than workers from Yorkshire do. Both groups need decent pay, stable housing and collective protection. What they lack is the institutional framework that would enforce those standards for everyone.

The programme proposed here creates that framework. Sectoral collective bargaining that enables workers to determine pay and conditions extensively in every area of the economy, public investment in housing and services that removes competition for scarce provision, full labour rights for all workers that prevent employers exploiting differential status, and migration tied to training that ensures labour supply expands as domestic training and capital investment are also expanding.

Under these conditions, workers can build solidarity on a material basis, that is, on common wage determination, protections, and access to services, rather than competing for scraps. The prospect of leaving capital free to move while workers compete against each other under deteriorating conditions is precisely the neoliberal settlement that the programme advocated in this book seeks to break. That is also the path towards a root and branch overhaul of the British economy, which is the crux of this book.

7

A Green Transition and the challenge of capital controls

7.1 Established interests

In late October 1936, Franklin Delano Roosevelt (FDR) addressed a rally at Madison Square Gardens in New York City as he campaigned to be re-elected president of the US. His speech outlined why he thought Americans had voted him into the White House at the depths of the Great Depression four years earlier – and why they should give him a second term.

Americans, FDR said, had opted in 1932 for 'peace of mind instead of gnawing fear'. They had sought escape from the personal terror that had stalked them in the three years following the Wall Street Crash of 1929. They had wanted security in their homes, safety for their savings, permanence in their jobs, and a fair day's pay for a fair day's work.

That was not all they wanted. US voters were capable of looking beyond their own circumstances and wanted to see their communities thrive, he said. A job and a decent income were important but so were schools, playgrounds, sanitation, highways – 'those things which are expected of solvent local government'.

At the national level, Americans sought – among other things – a stable US dollar, a shorter working week, the abolition of child labour and the elimination of the speculation that had been responsible for the Great Depression in the first place. Finally, Americans wanted peace in the world of unrest that existed in the 1930s. 'The Nation knows that I hate war, and I know that the Nation hates war.'

FDR stressed in his speech that progress had required struggle. His New Deal administration had been forced to battle against the opponents of change or as the president put it, 'the old enemies of peace: business and financial monopoly, speculation, reckless banking, class antagonism, sectionalism, war profiteering. They had begun to consider the government of the United States as a mere appendage to their own affairs. We know now that government by organised money is just as dangerous as government by organised mob. Never before in all our history have these forces been so united against one candidate as they stand today. They are unanimous in their hate for me – and I welcome their hatred.'

7.2 For a Green Transition

In retrospect, Roosevelt's repudiation of war was ironic since it was America's mobilisation of a war economy that ultimately brought the Great Depression to an end. Even so, the rest of his analysis of the US psyche in 1932 has a resonance in the Britain of 2026 – and contains important lessons for any government serious about bringing about the changes the country needs.

Economic security, safer and flourishing public spaces, better working conditions: these are still the things that people have the right to expect even though they have been notable by their absence for the past two decades.

FDR could hardly be described as a radical left winger. Brought up in a patrician family, he was by instinct a moderate; like Keynes he was intent not on destroying capitalism but of saving capitalism from itself. Even so, the contrast with the current breed of politicians is stark, especially in Roosevelt's willingness to do battle with big finance. Tony Blair's governments took pride in their light touch regulation of the financial sector and made London the go-to place for those seeking to push the boundaries beyond what had previously been considered acceptable and prudent. Supervision was only tightened when it was too late and the damage had been done.

By the likely date of the next British general election, a century will have passed since the Wall Street Crash of 1929 and the world is already a different place. With global heating becoming an ever-more potent threat, any plan for economic recovery that lacks a green dimension will fail the most basic sustainability test. Policy makers in the 1930s were able to ignore the environmental consequences of their growth strategies, with the need to reduce unemployment and tackle poverty the over-riding considerations. Today we do not have that luxury and must take the future of the planet into account.

The case for a radical New Deal for Britain is as powerful today as it was in the USA in the early 1930s. Harnessing the power of the state to lift economies out of prolonged stagnation, to give work to idle hands, to invest in new infrastructure: these are enduring ideas. They now need to be given a modern slant. Capitalism has been treating nature like an occupied country and is squeezing the life out of it. What is needed is a Green Transition.

7.3 The hoax of climate change denial

The Earth's temperature has been rising steadily since the middle of the nineteenth century, with the rate of increase accelerating since the early 1980s. The ten warmest years on record occurred in the decade 2015–24, with 2024 being the hottest. Britain's famously hot summer of 1976 would no longer make it into a list of the top five warmest. Global heating is a reality that can neither be ignored nor downplayed, and scientific evidence points to the emissions of CO_2 gas.

Historically, rich Western nations have accounted for the bulk of CO_2 emissions, even though poorer developing countries are most vulnerable to the effects of climate change. Britain has only managed to reduce its CO_2 emissions in recent years by outsourcing its manufacturing and energy production to other parts of the world. This is the first clue to how capitalism systematically evades environmental responsibility: production and its emissions are simply relocated rather than reduced.

Trump and his Make America Great Again supporters think climate change is either a hoax or not as serious as the scientists claim. Whereas his predecessor Joe Biden provided incentives for green manufacturing in the US, Trump's energy policy deliberately increases dependency on fossil fuels, and encourages other countries to do the same. By putting short-term cheap energy above sustainability – Trump's growth-at-any-cost strategy has put him on a collision course with the future of the planet.

7.4 Capitalism and the environmental crisis

The climate crisis is not an accident or a failure of individual choices. It is the predictable outcome of capitalism's basic logic. Capitalism treats nature as a free input and a free dumping ground for waste and emissions. The drive to maximise profits means externalising environmental costs onto society and future generations.

Neoliberalism made this systemic problem far worse. By freeing capital from national controls, it gave firms the ability to relocate production wherever environmental regulations were weakest and labour cheapest. The result has been a global race to the bottom. Countries compete to attract mobile capital by weakening environmental standards. Firms engage in carbon arbitrage – moving high-emissions production to jurisdictions with lax rules, then importing the products back. Britain's apparent emissions reductions are partly accounting tricks achieved by offshoring dirty production to China and elsewhere. Meanwhile, financial capital has poured trillions into fossil fuel extraction, power generation, and other carbon-intensive activities. These investments are not yet worthless ('stranded assets'), but they are exposed to growing risk as climate damage mounts, technologies change, and governments face pressure to act. That is precisely why capital reacts so aggressively when regulation is proposed. Firms threaten to move, financial markets raise borrowing costs, and investors demand protection against losses that would arise from their own long-term bets on fossil fuels. The power of these interests is a major obstacle to any serious transition.

Faced with this threat, environmental groups have found it hard to come up with a unified approach to the challenge of climate change. One wing of the movement – we might call them the Deep Greens – say the answer is de-growth and redistribution. The relentless pursuit of growth, they argue, has not made people happier, and the way ahead is to share the Earth's resources more equitably. They are right that capitalism's growth imperative on a finite planet is unsustainable. They are also right that GDP growth has been decoupled from genuine wellbeing.

But telling deindustrialised regions and precarious workers to accept less is politically dead on arrival. Thus far, there is little evidence that making people poorer has made them more willing to tackle the climate crisis. On the contrary, the squeeze on living standards has pushed the environment down the list of voter priorities and fostered a growth-at-all-costs mentality in government.

The issue is not growth as such but what grows and who benefits from it. A transformed economy can expand production of renewable energy, retrofit millions of homes for energy efficiency, build public transport systems, and manufacture heat pumps – all of which increase material output and employment while reducing emissions. At the same time, fossil fuel extraction, private jet travel, and planned obsolescence in consumer goods can shrink. The composition of the economy changes, not simply its scale.

Growth is not an end in itself but rather a means to deliver real wealth creation: better homes, cleaner rivers and beaches; incomes sufficient to obviate the need for food banks and cities not choked with pollution. Developing new manufacturing and applications generates new techniques, skills and knowledge and thereby enriches scientific understanding that can be deployed to minimise environmental damage and foster creative solutions.

7.5 Why market solutions fail

The neoliberal response to climate change has been to create market mechanisms – carbon trading schemes, emissions offsets, green finance assets. These have manifestly failed. Carbon markets allow continued emissions while generating speculative profits for traders. Offsets let polluters pay for theoretical emissions reductions elsewhere rather than cutting their own. Corporate Net Zero pledges are mostly 'greenwashing' tricks that change nothing fundamental.

Market-based approaches systematically put costs on ordinary people, while letting capital escape. Energy bills rise for households. Taxes on fuel hit workers who commute. Meanwhile, the largest polluters continue operating, their emissions grandfathered into cap-and-trade systems or offset through dubious accounting.

The problem is not that fossil fuel assets are already stranded, but that they remain profitable under existing rules. Capital follows returns, not long-term social need. Fossil fuel infrastructure is already built, enjoys regulated or geopolitically protected markets, and delivers predictable cash flows backed by decades of subsidy and state support. That is why private investment continues to flow into oil, gas and carbon-intensive activity even as the environmental damage mounts. The market is behaving exactly as capitalism dictates. A green transition will not emerge spontaneously from price signals. It requires the state to change the rules, redirect investment, and override profit logic where it conflicts with social survival

When Rachel Reeves gave the annual Mansion House speech to the massed ranks of the UK financial sector in July 2025, she made it clear that Labour had no intention of forcing the issue. Where Roosevelt had welcomed the 'hate' of Wall Street, Reeves agreed with those in the City of London pressing for deregulation of finance. 'In too many areas, regulation still acts as a boot on the neck of businesses, choking off the enterprise and innovation that is the lifeblood of growth', she said. Her concessions to finance are a profound mistake. As in the 1930s, real change won't happen until the freedom of capital is curtailed.

7.6 Capital controls and the Green Transition

All of this is possible but none of it will happen unless one key lesson of the original New Deal is learned: the need to control and direct private capital. Roosevelt understood that national recovery meant putting Wall Street under tight supervision and regulation, which was why his first few months in the White House saw a flurry of legislative action to curb the power of financial capital. The Emergency Banking act gave him the authorisation to regulate banks and foreign exchange transactions, and to reorganise or close banks. The creation of the Federal Deposit Insurance Corporation ensured that depositors' savings were protected. The Glass–Steagall Act split commercial banking from investment banking in an attempt to prevent speculation derailing the financial system and the wider economy.

These curbs were kept in place after the Second World War, providing post-war governments with the ability to pursue domestic economic goals without the fear of speculative attack from finance. It was no accident that the first three decades after 1945 saw rates of growth and investment not equalled let alone surpassed before or since. It was also a period marked by the absence of financial crises.

Capital controls are essential for a Green Transition because they restore democratic capacity to implement what science requires. They prevent firms from escaping environmental regulation by relocating production. They stop bond markets from punishing governments that act decisively on climate. They ensure that patient, long-term investment flows to green infrastructure rather than short-term speculation. They allow each country to impose strict environmental standards without fear of an immediate capital exodus.

As the years passed and memories of the Wall Street crash faded, finance started to pressure governments to relax the constraints on their activities. Free movement of money capital, it was argued, would make capital more efficient, since the markets would always be better at seeking out profitable investment opportunities than governments. Social democratic parties gradually abandoned their belief in capital controls invariably using the power of global financial forces as an excuse for their own timidity. It came as little surprise to find that when Wall Street finally managed to have Glass–Steagall repealed in 1999, it was at the hands of Bill Clinton, a Democrat president. To this day, unhindered capital movement remains one of the EU's four freedoms.

The neoliberal rationale for letting finance out of its post-war cage was that it would make capital more abundant, and that investment would boom as a result. This was supposed to be true internationally as well as domestically, with the removal of capital being a central theme of the neoliberal Washington consensus orchestrated by the International Monetary Fund and the US Treasury. We now know that the outcome was disastrous for both people and planet. Capital must be controlled, if there is to be wealth creation for the many and if the climate and environmental crisis is to be tackled. Yet two objections are routinely raised against this conclusion.

It is often objected that capital controls only work with international coordination, or that they imply crude bans on capital leaving the country. Neither claim is correct. International cooperation, such as the Bretton Woods framework that governed capital movements in the first three decades after the Second World War, can make controls more effective, but it has never been a precondition for their use. States have repeatedly acted unilaterally to manage capital flows when domestic priorities required it, including in advanced economies.

Capital controls are not a single instrument but a graduated set of mechanisms, ranging from transaction taxes and holding-period requirements to licensing regimes and targeted restrictions on specific flows. Their purpose is not to halt all cross-border finance, but to change incentives, slow destabilising movements, and restore policy space. Like any powerful instrument, controls carry risks, especially in a highly financialised economy such as Britain's. How those risks can be managed, and how controls can be designed to work in the UK context, is taken up explicitly in the strategy chapters that follow.

7.7 Capital controls are perfectly feasible

China is the prime example of a country that has flouted the neoliberal orthodoxy and operated tough controls on capital, together with foreign exchange intervention, to reduce macro-economic volatility and enable the government to pursue domestic goals: rapid industrialisation, managed investment and high levels of employment. Any easing of capital controls has been carefully calibrated and modest. China has recognised what neoliberals in the West appear to have forgotten: that capital needs to be managed if it is to be effectively used. Given the difference between China's growth rate and that of the US – the G7's best performing economy – policy makers in Beijing are unlikely to heed lectures from Western neoliberals that capital controls are harming the economy.

But China is not the only country to use capital controls. Chile imposed reserve requirements – effectively a tax – and minimum stay requirements on capital inflows in order to prevent inflows of speculative money from destabilising the economy. Other countries that have used capital controls include Brazil, Malaysia, Thailand, and many more.

One long mooted control on capital is a financial transaction tax, an idea originally proposed by the US economist James Tobin in the early 1970s – a Tobin tax. Originally conceived as a levy on foreign exchange dealings, modern forms have been broadened to include other financial instruments, such as derivatives. Even in the days when capital controls were still in extensive use, Tobin said there was a need to throw 'sand in the wheels' of currency markets to limit the extent to which speculators could force governments to change economic policy. The size, scope and power of finance have all increased significantly since the 1970s, making such controls even more necessary.

Despite the obvious benefits, resistance to a Tobin tax has been strong, particularly in the West's two main financial centres, the USA and the UK. But there are no valid technical arguments against the imposition of such a tax since all financial transactions are logged with a digital footprint. Nor can it be said that a levy on finance is a radical new idea, since the UK has had a stamp duty imposed on share dealings for centuries, which is a kind of financial transaction tax. Stamp duties are impossible to evade, and British governments have found them to be a reliable source of revenue. A broader financial transaction tax – even if levied at a fraction of one per cent – would prove even more lucrative and could help fund a Green Transition.

Other controls of a similar character are also available. It would be possible, for instance, to oblige UK pension funds – which receive £70b a year in government tax breaks – to invest a quarter of their new contributions in UK growth assets including green infrastructure rather than channelling them overseas. As the pension campaigner Ros Altmann has noted, pension managers and trustees used to invest most of their assets in equities, with very high allocations to shares listed in London. But in recent years, funds have steadily reduced their exposure to Britain, damaging growth prospects by cutting off a vital source of investment. Britain has one of the largest pools of long-term investment assets in the world, but only a small fraction is directed towards domestic productive investment, and even less towards green infrastructure. The government, meanwhile, provides tax relief for pension managers to invest in other countries rather than our own.

7.8 What the Green Transition requires

The Green New Deal – which first came to prominence at the time of the Great Crisis – sought to marry economic recovery with environmental action. The idea was to update the original New Deal to meet the needs of the twenty-first century, so instead of building new dams and motorways, the Green New Deal proposed providing well-paid jobs in every constituency by employing local people to retrofit their homes with energy-saving insulation.

Over half of Britain's homes – around 18m – have poor energy efficiency, with an energy performance certificate of D or lower. Homes with a very poor rating of F end up with huge energy bills, in excess of £4,000 per year. Those bills could be cut by more than half if retrofitting homes raised that rating to a C, making a material difference to hard-pressed households.

Improving the state of Britain's housing stock would form one strand of an industrial strategy in which the government identifies potential growth sectors and puts serious funding behind the development of environmentally friendly technologies. This cannot be achieved through market signals alone. It requires public investment at scale, coordination across supply chains, trained workforce with portable skills, and long-term finance willing to accept patient returns rather than speculative gains.

That is precisely what free capital movement prevents. Without controls, firms prefer short-term returns over patient green investment. Training programmes go underfunded because mobile capital won't commit to staying long enough to benefit. Supply chains fragment as production relocates to wherever costs are momentarily lowest. The patient coordinated investment necessary for home retrofit at scale simply doesn't materialise.

Capital controls make it possible. They ensure investment stays domestic. They allow government to direct pension funds towards green infrastructure. They prevent firms from escaping environmental regulation. They create the stable conditions necessary for workers to acquire skills knowing there will be jobs to use them.

Harnessing the expertise of universities and encouraging spin-offs from academia would be vital to divert resources away from polluting activities and into the Net Zero transition. But again, this requires more than good intentions. University research in clean technology is pointless if capital flows immediately to offshore manufacturing. Spin-offs fail if venture capital demands quick exits rather than patient support for scaling up production. The innovation ecosystem needs capital controls to function effectively.

7.9 Political will and determination

The swift government responses to both the Great Crisis and the pandemic crisis delivered a fatal blow to the argument that a Green Transition is unaffordable. Confronted with the grave risk of complete economic collapse, governments soon found enormous amounts of money – spent whatever it took – to avoid a second Great Depression and paid no heed to fiscal orthodoxy.

This made sense since a country that commands its own currency, and its debt is largely denominated in it, can borrow funds and create money to keep activity going. Britain cannot be forced into insolvency as long as it controls its currency and the denomination of its debt; the real constraints are political and distributional, not financial. If the British government thought climate change was a serious enough threat it would find the necessary resources to act.

Since the short-lived disastrous government led by Liz Truss in 2022, both Conservative and Labour governments have pursued ultra-orthodox monetary and fiscal policies for fear of a backlash from the financial markets. In its own strange way, the seven-week Truss premiership illustrates our central argument: without controls on capital politicians are forced to operate within the confines of what the markets consider to be appropriate.

Labour was running scared of the 'bond market vigilantes' even while it was in opposition. It scaled back the declared ambition of its green prosperity plan to show to the City of London that it was serious about meeting the fiscal rules laid down by Rachel Reeves, who became its Chancellor. The obeisance to the City lives on after the formation of the Labour government.

It is impossible to imagine Rachel Reeves or Keir Starmer saying: 'I am hated by the City and I welcome that hate', but it would be a sign of tremendous progress if leading people in British government did precisely that.

Britain needs to transform its economy and society in the direction of wealth creation in the interests of working people. It also needs to engage in a Green Transition, at the very least attempting to meet the target of Net Zero, which is now a legal obligation of the British government, after all. None of that is possible without a radical strategy for change that incorporates Net Zero, promotes public ownership and investment, and seeks to control both trade and capital flows.

7.10 The AI infrastructure trap

The green transition faces an additional threat from an unexpected quarter: the explosive growth of artificial intelligence infrastructure. In January 2025, the Labour government unveiled its AI Opportunities Action Plan, promising to 'turbocharge AI' and make Britain an 'AI powerhouse'. The strategy explicitly relies on crowding in private capital – overwhelmingly US – to build massive data centres across the country.

The scale is staggering. Blackstone, the US private equity giant, is developing a £10 billion AI data centre campus in Blyth, Northumberland. US-based Vantage Data Centres is building a £12 billion facility in Wales. Google DeepMind, OpenAI, Microsoft, and Meta all have major operations in Britain. The government has created 'AI Growth Zones' with enhanced access to power and streamlined planning to facilitate these developments.

The energy demands are immense. A single hyperscale data campus can draw between 100 and 500 megawatts, consuming several terawatt-hours each year. These sites use vast amounts of electricity – directly competing with the power needed to electrify transport and heating, both essential for reaching Net Zero. They also require huge volumes of water for cooling. To put this in perspective, a 500-megawatt facility uses roughly as much power as around one to two million homes. Overall demand could rise from around 800 gigawatt-hours to as much as 4,000 gigawatt-hours per year – the difference between the electricity use of a city twice the size of Coventry and one larger than Birmingham. By 2030, AI data centres could even account for around seven per cent of total UK electricity consumption.

The huge energy demand creates multiple problems that capital controls together with public ownership and energy planning could address. First, US ownership means profits flow abroad while Britain bears infrastructure costs and environmental burdens. Second, US law reaches extraterritorially through legislation like the CLOUD Act, giving US authorities access to data stored in Britain regardless of UK law. Third, the energy consumption locks in demand that competes with green transition priorities.

But the deeper issue is who controls technological development and for what purpose. The current approach serves finance capital and US tech giants. Data centres are built not because they meet social needs but because they generate profits for Silicon Valley. The vast computational resources go towards training AI models owned by foreign corporations, not addressing climate change or rebuilding productive capacity.

More fundamentally, Britain needs democratic control over technological development. Public ownership of digital infrastructure, like public ownership of energy systems, ensures decisions serve social purpose. Without such control, AI development will continue to be shaped by capital's priorities: profit extraction and speculation rather than genuine wealth creation or environmental sustainability. The freedom of capital to build what it wants, where it wants, using Britain's scarce energy and water resources, is incompatible with both green transition and national sovereignty.

Part II

A Strategy For Wealth Creation – What To Do

8

Six steps for wealth creation

For decades there has been a thriving cottage industry in books pointing out what needs to be done to revive the economy. The first of them appeared when Britain was still the workshop of the world in the mid-nineteenth century but there was concern about the threat posed by countries such as Germany, which had better-trained and better-educated workers. Books that go beyond the merely descriptive and explain what needs to be done to arrest the decline have been thinner on the ground.

This chapter and the three that follow seek to put this right and form the core of our book. Here we move from diagnosis to prescription, from critique to construction. What follows is detailed, sometimes technical, but necessarily so. Reindustrialisation cannot be achieved through slogans or vague commitments to 'industrial strategy'. It requires setting quantitative targets, calculating labour needs, estimating investment levels and sequencing, evaluating energy constraints, proposing new institutional design, and incorporating environmental and climate considerations.

8.1 Getting on the right side of history

Those who benefited most from the plundering of the British economy and the resulting extreme inequality have no credible plan to offer. Yet the British people recognise that the country desperately needs a different course. Trade unions in partnership with the many organisations of the public sphere should help create a new vision with concrete proposals. The aim is straightforward: to rebuild the capacity to create wealth while shifting social and economic power from capital to labour so that wealth can be shared for the benefit of all.

The task requires a sustained increase in the productivity of labour. But for productivity to rise, Britain needs a larger, stronger industrial base – above all, a revival of manufacturing. Given the lopsided structure of the British economy, there is no other reliable route to broad and sustained productivity gains. Reindustrialising Britain will be a first in modern economic history: the original industrialiser attempting to reindustrialise. It will be difficult, but it is necessary.

Labour supply is the first constraint. Earlier industrialisers drew workers from the peasantry or from large pools of urban underemployment; Britain has neither. Industry must reorganise the existing workforce, bring through young entrants at scale, and – where needed – admit migrant labour with full protection and rights. That requires a serious training system with real capacity: college places and apprenticeships, and structured on-the-job programmes tied to actual openings, not token schemes.

Economic and social power must also shift in favour of labour, which means that wages must rise, working conditions must improve, and skills must be improved systematically. Workers need stronger organisation and an independent voice in public life. Democratic citizenship and popular sovereignty must be recast to integrate non-UK-born workers as full participants in the economy. Without this, the class settlement that has led the country to the current impasse will not change.

External conditions now favour this drastic change of approach. For decades the Washington Consensus – free trade and free movement of money capital – gave multinationals and big finance a free hand. Since 2007–9 that model of capitalism has frayed and managed trade has returned. In 2025 the Trump Administration in the USA made that explicit with sweeping tariffs outside WTO discipline. Many countries also use capital controls – rules that slow or stop short-term money flows – to protect domestic investment and stabilise exchange rates.

China has shown that an alternative route to neoliberal capitalism is available: state-led industrial policy, large public corporations, protected domestic markets, and tight control over capital and the exchange rate. Its manufacturing base is larger than those of the USA, Japan, and Germany combined. The rise of the BRICS (Brazil, Russia, India, China and South Africa) has reinforced this shift: in 2023, they accounted for about thirty-five per cent of world manufacturing value added (roughly twenty-eight per cent in China alone), a share comparable to the USA and EU taken together (about seventeen per cent in USA and eighteen per cent in the EU).

8.2 Space and constraints

These global shifts create space for a complete change of direction in Britain. Our main trading partners remain the EU and the USA, but the USA has abandoned free-trade orthodoxy, and the UK is not bound by EU rules after Brexit. Britain can adopt a range of policies, including targeted trade measures and sensible capital controls to support reindustrialisation on its own terms.

Doing so requires confronting British capital directly. The point is to curb the power of the social class that built and still defends the current failed model, assert national and popular sovereignty, reject the ghost of empire still haunting public life, and refuse to ally Britain with attempts to re-impose US hegemony across the world.

Climate is also a binding constraint. Reindustrialisation must cut emissions and clean up the environment – tasks that profit-first capitalism has repeatedly failed to deliver. Britain has the research base, the technologies, and the public backing to build a clean industry if the state leads and sets the pace.

The central focus remains reindustrialisation. This will enable Britain to shift income and power towards labour and at the same time act internationally in the interests of workers. It requires delivering measurable results on a clear timetable, while grounding legitimacy in the needs of British people. That calls for a political and social movement prepared for conflict and institution-building.

8.3 Concrete objectives

A credible strategy must begin with a hard look at where British manufacturing currently stands and how it compares with peer economies. Germany and Italy are the relevant European benchmarks – not because they have done well in recent years, but because, amid Europe's wider decline, they still retain sizeable manufacturing bases, as is clear from Table 8.1:

Table 8.1 Manufacturing in Germany, Italy and Britain, 2023–4

Country	Share of GDP (%)	Employment (millions)	Share of total Employment (%)
Germany	19	7.9	19
Italy	15	3.9	16
Britain	8	2.6	8

Source: Own calculations based on World Bank, ONS (UK), ISTAT (LFS; *Rapporto annuale* series; Italy), Destatis and OECD LFS (Germany).

These numbers help us avoid setting fantasy targets. Britain stands no chance of reaching German levels in ten years, and matching Italy would imply almost doubling manufacturing's GDP share, which is also impossible during the same period. The plan that follows therefore treats Germany and Italy as reference points but sets a modest, workable objective: raise Britain's manufacturing share to a minimum of eleven per cent of GDP over a decade.

The point of the target is not to fetishise a threshold, but to show how a realistic goal would materially change the country to the benefit of the British people. We could set the target at twelve or thirteen per cent, and both might be achievable with an even greater effort, but the thrust of the strategy would remain the same. It is better, then, to pursue the analysis with the more modest target of eleven per cent. Since this would merely return manufacturing to its share of GDP at the time of the Great Crisis it suffices to show that reindustrialisation is perfectly feasible in the UK and allows us to outline in detail the necessary steps.

8.4 Priorities

To make sense of what must be built, it helps to split manufacturing into four groups:

(i) Foundational: metal products, chemicals, plastics, basic metals (steel, aluminium), cement, paper, oil refining.
(ii) Enabling: machine tools, computers and electronics, electrical equipment.
(iii) Advanced: pharmaceuticals, motor vehicles, other transport (air/ship/rail), advanced electronics and materials, robotics.
(iv) Consumer: food, textiles and leather, printing, furniture.

These groups are of roughly equal weight inside today's manufacturing sector; with manufacturing at about eight per cent of GDP in 2023–4, each group accounts for about two per cent. Foundational industries matter most for scale: steel, aluminium, chemicals, and cement feed almost every production chain. A similar logic applies to enabling industries – machine tools, electronics and electrical equipment – without which both foundational and advanced sectors stall.

Herein lies Britain's real weakness: Deindustrialisation since the Thatcher years devastated the foundational and enabling base. From a global producer in the 1970s, Britain has become marginal. As proportions of her GDP, steel and aluminium are around 0.2 per cent, cement less than 0.3 per cent, machine tools less than 0.7 per cent. In 2023, Germany produced roughly 36 million metric tonnes of steel and Italy twenty million, while Britain produced about 5.6 million. China, meanwhile, produced more than 1,000 million.

Advanced manufacturing looks marginally better. Britain retains global strengths in aerospace and automobiles (the latter largely foreign owned), plus pharmaceuticals and some advanced materials. Much of this rests on significant R&D, often linked to universities which, despite funding strains and over-reliance on foreign students, still hold strong research positions globally. This is an asset for reindustrialisation, yet without a domestic foundational and enabling base for manufacturing these strengths depend on imports and foreign corporate strategies, leaving the whole system highly exposed.

The objective is clear: rebuild foundational and enabling industries, while expanding existing niches in advanced manufacturing. Furthermore, there are two further infrastructural mechanisms that do not belong to manufacturing directly but are vital for its revival energy and transport. Rebuilding energy and transport will make it easier to rebuild manufacturing.

Developing the appropriate strategy is a difficult task requiring political will, national mobilisation, and a readiness to confront the social interests that cling to the status quo. But the difference with the current Labour government's approach is already apparent. The strategy we propose treats manufacturing as an integral whole – a system – rather than as a collection of sectors that happen to have higher productivity than others. It is a system that requires the right infrastructure to function successfully, and there are weaknesses that have to be addressed.

8.5 The realities of energy

Energy in Britain spans upstream oil and gas extraction (mining), oil refining (manufacturing), and utilities (electricity and gas; water and sewerage). Electricity generation is dominated by gas, nuclear, and renewables. Oil is marginal to power generation but remains central to transport and – alongside gas – to heating. Water and sewerage matter for food processing and chemicals, but their economy-wide impact on manufacturing is modest and can be set aside for now.

Reindustrialisation is inseparable from energy. Manufacturing depends on power that is secure, affordable, and reliable, yet Britain enters any programme of industrial renewal with a weakened and fragmented energy system. Decades of privatisation, market fragmentation, and under-investment have left the country unusually exposed to volatile prices, import dependence, and weak coordination between generation, networks, and industrial demand.

The energy price shock since 2021 exposed these vulnerabilities starkly. Energy-intensive sectors such as steel, chemicals, fertilisers, paper, glass and ceramics faced sharp cost increases and supply uncertainty, contributing to output losses, temporary shutdowns and permanent closures. These pressures reflected an energy system organised around short-term wholesale markets and financial returns rather than long-term industrial needs. Britain's heavy reliance on imported fuels, particularly gas, means that international price shocks pass rapidly into domestic electricity prices, directly affecting manufacturing costs.

For industry, the issue is not simply the average price of electricity but the combination of system capacity, predictable pricing, and the ability to connect, expand, and operate continuously. That depends on adequate generation margins, investment in transmission and distribution networks, and system-balancing arrangements capable of managing variable supply without exposing producers to sudden price spikes or interruption risk. Weak gas storage, limited grid capacity in key regions, and fragmented investment decisions have become binding constraints on industrial activity.

These structural weaknesses are mirrored in the shrinking direct economic weight of energy. Today the energy complex accounts for only a low single-digit share of Gross Value Added (GVA), a fraction of what it represented during the era when coal and North Sea oil formed pillars of Britain's productive base. GVA captures the value generated in production and is therefore the relevant measure when assessing industrial structure and capacity; GDP, by contrast, folds in taxes and subsidies and tells us less about where value is actually created. The collapse of energy's economic weight since the early 1980s is a defining feature of British neoliberal capitalism. It reflects two decisive ruptures, namely the destruction of coal mining after the 1984–85 Miners' Strike and the long decline of North Sea oil following its peak at the end of the twentieth century.

Britain is now a net energy importer, with gas the major fuel. In refined oil, it imports just over half of domestic demand and exports nearly as much, leaving only a modest net dependency. Britain imports roughly half of the gas it consumes, a stark reversal from the era of North Sea self-sufficiency. It has no uranium mines and imports virtually all its uranium ore, though enrichment takes place partly at domestic facilities. Renewables are domestically generated, except for biomass, and now provide half of UK electricity generation, yet price formation remains tied to gas. Electricity imports typically supply around fifteen per cent of demand, depending on the year.

Ownership and control have also shifted abroad. A substantial share of North Sea oil and gas licences is held by foreign firms. Nuclear generation is almost entirely operated by EDF, the French state utility. Foreign ownership pervades power generation, particularly offshore wind, where project ownership is dominated by non-UK firms. Transmission and distribution networks operate as regulated monopolies and include significant foreign-owned operators. Revenues raised from British industry and households therefore flow steadily overseas rather than being reinvested domestically.

The outcome is predictable. Britain pays among the highest electricity prices in Europe for industry, while household prices are also above the EU average. Gas sets the marginal power price, with more than half supplied by pipeline from Norway and the remainder as liquefied natural gas from the United States and Qatar. Global gas price spikes therefore feed directly into UK electricity prices. These effects are amplified by Britain's exceptionally limited gas storage capacity, which is tiny by European standards, leaving the country acutely exposed to winter price spikes.

The legal commitment to Net Zero emissions by 2050 tightens these constraints further. Decarbonisation requires large-scale, coordinated investment in generation, grids, storage, and system management, alongside electrification of transport, heating and parts of industry. Without coordination, the transition risks higher costs, bottlenecks and instability. With coordination, it offers the prospect of lower long-run energy costs, reduced exposure to imported fuels and greater system resilience.

Energy policy therefore cannot be reduced to a single technological choice. Reindustrialisation requires an energy system capable of delivering sufficient scale, continuous supply, predictable prices, and public control. In the short and medium term, this necessarily involves a mix of generation sources. Gas will not disappear overnight given existing infrastructure and heating systems. Renewables must expand rapidly but require complementary investment in grids and storage. Nuclear power may play a role in providing firm low-carbon capacity, but only under conditions that meet wider requirements of cost, delivery speed, domestic capability and ownership.

Delivery mechanisms matter as much as technology choices. Renewables expansion depends on manufacturing capacity for turbines, panels and inverters, much of which Britain currently imports. Grid investment requires domestic capability in high-voltage equipment, transformers and cabling. Nuclear programmes, whether large-scale plants or small modular reactors, need construction skills, regulatory frameworks, and supply chains that Britain has largely lost. In each case, the strategic question is whether investment rebuilds domestic capability or simply imports equipment and expertise while profits flow overseas. Great British Energy, with adequate capital and clear public ownership, can act as developer and coordinator across these technologies, anchoring investment decisions in industrial policy rather than financial speculation.

The central issue is not which technology is preferred, but who controls the system and for what purpose. In short, Britain lacks energy sovereignty, and the cost and insecurity of power undermine both industrial competitiveness and living standards. Some clear ideas on how to tackle the problem have come from the trade union movement. Unite the Union has, for instance, proposed re-nationalisation beginning with the grid (both transmission and distribution networks), a significant pay rise for energy workers, proper funding for GB Energy, a public stake in green energy projects, and a truly just transition for North Sea workers as the UK moves to Net Zero. Any coherent strategy of reindustrialisation must incorporate measures of this kind to expand, secure and cheapen domestic power, treating energy as a foundational input to wealth creation rather than a speculative commodity.

8.6 Transport and the importance of rail

The transport sector, which is also critical to reindustrialisation, has a highly fragmented ownership. Roads are publicly owned, but haulage fleets are entirely private. Rail infrastructure is public (Network Rail), while rail freight is private, and passenger services are a mix of private concessions and a few public operators. Buses outside London are deregulated and privately run; in London, services are specified and funded by Transport for London but operated by private contractors. Ports are overwhelmingly private and largely foreign-owned; airports, too, are mostly in foreign hands. Fragmentation raises costs and weakens reliability compared with the more integrated, publicly anchored systems of Germany and Italy.

Congestion is also characteristic of the British transport system and means higher costs. Cars dominate passenger travel in Britain, accounting for well over three-quarters of passenger miles. Freight traffic also relies heavily on roads. Yet Britain's motorway network is far smaller than Germany's and significantly smaller than Italy's. There are bottlenecks and delays across both motorways and main roads.

Freight depends heavily on road transport, which is bad for both the environment and efficiency. By tonne-kilometres, road haulage carries about eighty per cent of domestic freight; rail freight accounts for roughly eight per cent and mainly moves bulk inputs such as steel, aggregates and chemicals; about twelve per cent moves by water (inland and coastal). In international trade, ports handle around ninety-five per cent of goods by weight. Air freight is a small share by volume but strategically important for high-value products such as pharmaceuticals, aerospace and electronics. Passenger rail and buses are critical for workforce mobility and therefore for productivity. Public transport outside London has declined sharply since 2009, damaging labour mobility across the Midlands, North and Wales.

Rail under-utilisation is another major source of inefficiency. Rail freight is cheaper per tonne-kilometre over long distances and less vulnerable to congestion, while road transport carries far higher carbon costs – an additional burden for British industry competing with Germany and Italy. Yet less than forty per cent of Britain's rail network is electrified, compared with about sixty per cent in Germany and over seventy per cent in Italy. Moreover, passenger fares remain among the highest in Europe, driving up commuting costs and wage pressure.

In sum, congestion and weak transport infrastructure push up costs, lengthen journeys, and force manufacturers to hold larger buffer stocks while risking missed port slots. Britain's smaller motorway network and lower rail-freight share inflate fuel and labour costs; limited bus services outside London reduce labour catchments and increase absenteeism.

Rebuilding the UK's wealth-creating capacity requires fixing these structural failures in transport, shifting power away from rent-seekers and back towards productive industry and labour. The legislation introduced by the Labour government in November 2025 to establish Great British Railways (GBR) – strongly backed by the RMT, the National Union of Rail, Maritime and Transport Workers – offers a concrete step in that direction.

Great British Railways is the planned national rail company intended to reunify the system under public ownership. It will be a state-owned enterprise managing most rail operations in Britain, excluding services such as Transport for London and Merseyrail. GBR will absorb the functions of Network Rail and the franchised train operators, bringing passenger services back into a single public framework for the first time since privatisation. The transition will be gradual, with contracts ending and operations returning to public control over time. GBR's creation marks a clear acknowledgement of the failure of rail privatisation and the need for public coordination.

It is a welcome reform and a genuine opportunity to confront the inefficiencies of fragmented ownership and outdated, narrow concepts of labour productivity. Productivity measures based solely on labour costs have dominated most sectors, including rail, leading to work intensification, job cuts, and fire-and-rehire practices. There is now a chance to reset these measures, as unions have long demanded, by adopting broader definitions of productivity such as those advocated by the Productivity Institute – ones that include budgetary and organisational efficiency and assess effectiveness in terms of social and economic contribution.

A fully nationalised rail system would also benefit from eliminating the wasteful transaction costs that have piled up over three decades of privatisation. Alongside the private-sector debt of Network Rail and the rising cost of leased rolling stock, multiple contractual interfaces have drained public funds and fare revenue while dragging down productivity. Removing these inefficiencies would allow rail to fulfil its full potential as a driver of economic growth.

Greater integration within rail should also support a new, fully funded national apprenticeship scheme offering industry-wide training, clear career pathways from school to retirement, and continuous skill development. Insourcing rail manufacturing and maintenance would reinforce this effort and provide a major boost to reindustrialisation.

8.7 A reindustrialisation strategy in six steps

In this light, Britain requires a strategy for reindustrialisation that would rebuild wealth creation over the medium to long term while tilting the social balance in favour of labour. Its objective would be to lift manufacturing's share of GDP from eight to eleven per cent by 2035, while creating foundations that allow further increases in the future. Benefits for working people and for the wider economy would begin to show soon after implementation.

The strategy we propose has the following six interconnected steps:

(i) Necessary labour
(ii) Public ownership
(iii) An investment wave

(iv) A public bank
(v) Trade regulation
(vi) Capital controls

The first three steps are analysed in Chapter 9 and the last three in Chapter 10. Our aim is not to forecast what is required with spurious precision but rather to demonstrate that a careful reindustrialisation strategy is perfectly feasible for Britain. We assume that the commitment to Net Zero – a legal commitment since 2019 – continues, even though in the short run it will make the task of boosting manufacturing's share of the economy more testing.

The strategy and the projections made in Part II are based on the realisation that British reindustrialisation represents a truly novel historical challenge. The issue facing us is not creating industrial capacity in a less developed and still heavily agrarian country but re-creating it in the country that was the first to industrialise and the first to de-industrialise to such a dramatic extent. Britain confronts the historical task of being the first to re-industrialise at scale after a sustained and deliberate dismantling of its industrial base. The strategy proposed here is capable of delivering on this task, boosting the country's wealth creation and providing a credible path towards Net Zero.[1]

[1] In technical terms, Britain's reindustrialisation is not a conventional late-development problem of scarce capital, surplus agrarian labour, and weak technology. It is the inverse: an advanced, financialised economy with mobile capital, a service-dominated labour force, and substantial residual technological capacity. The macroeconomic framework underlying our projections draws on the Kalecki–Kaldor analysis of aggregate demand and aggregate supply and on Marx's analysis of accumulation and distribution, treating investment, profitability and effective demand as jointly determining output and employment. For accounting consistency we assume a stable capital–output relationship. The numerical magnitudes presented in Part II are not generated by solving the formal model but from transparent accounting assumptions consistent with this framework. The formal theoretical structure is set out in a separate SOAS Department of Economics Working Paper.

9

Labour, nationalisation and investment

Step 1. Necessary labour

9.1 Increase in employment

The past half century has seen the steady decline in manufacturing as a share of the economy, so even a modest reversal of that trend will take some doing. It will require not just more people working in factories, but better trained workers using up to date equipment so that they are more productive. Under these conditions, a return to a sustained annual growth rate of 2.75 per cent is feasible, which is the macroeconomic assumption underpinning the plan. Manufacturing productivity is assumed to rise by 3.5 per cent a year – again ambitious yet historically achievable.

The first requirement is labour because without the right workers with the right skills the manufacturing recovery simply won't happen. Current manufacturing employment is roughly 2.6 million and even assuming higher productivity that won't be sufficient to hit the eleven per cent of GDP target. To do that will require close to 725,000 net additional workers. Once allowance has been made for those retiring, gross hiring will be around one million workers over the next decade – or 100,000 new recruits a year.

The UK population is just over 69 million and a falling birth rate means natural growth is negligible, which explains why recent growth in the workforce has been driven mainly by migration. The bulk of the required labour must come from three sources: the economically inactive, workers shifting out of other sectors, and a planned migration component. A workable annual split is fifty-five thousand from other sectors, thirty thousand from inactivity, and fifteen thousand through targeted migration.

Allocation of the additional labour force by sector will be important. Manufacturing has to grow and that expansion needs to shift towards foundational and enabling industries. It is reasonable to expect these two groups to absorb more than half of the increase of labour. Consequently, there will be skills in short supply, including welders and metal fabricators; toolmakers; electrical and instrumentation technicians; Computer Numerical Control programmers; mechatronics, automation and robotics technicians; and a range of engineers. These skills will not appear by themselves: Britain must train its young as they enter the labour force and retrain those shifting from other sectors. A plan for the labour force is needed, such as Britain has not had for decades.

9.2 Wages and skills

Two crucial elements are immediately clear. First, wages must rise to attract workers where new capacity is created. Tight labour supply will do part of the job, but policy must also raise wage floors in manufacturing and end the long squeeze on wages that has blighted the British economy. Higher wages should act as an incentive to draw people out of inactivity and to support higher productivity.

It is also worth stressing that public sector pay is not a cost that the government must strive continually to reduce.

On the contrary, it is an economic incentive that can pay for itself through improved efficiency helping to boost growth and the tax yield, as public sector unions have repeatedly argued.

Second, training must improve and expand. The initial emphasis would be on shop-floor skills, with a steady shift to more complex roles as automation spreads. Britain needs long programmes, mid-career conversions, short courses, and apprenticeships with high completion rates. The current institutions are not yet fit for purpose: systems are fragmented, funding is unstable, and technical education has been crowded out by mass higher education. England is particularly weak on post-sixteen-years higher technical routes, which are fundamental to contemporary economies.

Artificial intelligence is likely to accelerate change. The exposure of office and process roles to AI is already visible – clerical processing, document review, routine procurement, payroll, basic data entry – and measured productivity effects are uneven and will take time. In the Civil Service (about 540,000 workers in 2024), pressure will be sharpest in large back-office and operational delivery functions (benefits, tax administration, licensing, etc.). It is likely that there will be a squeeze on lower and some middle grades where work is text-heavy and rules-based. What is needed is a plan for redeployment of workers opting to remain as well as retraining of those who will seek employment in the new sectors. Without such planning, the result will be a reduction in the number of workers, eroding state capability rather than raising it.

Similar considerations extend across the broader service sector: finance and insurance, retail and logistics, customer operations, professional services, education administration, and healthcare administration. Unlike in the past, the jobs most vulnerable to AI are not low-skilled. Redeployment and retraining must be deliberate, funded, and meet industry demand, with apprenticeships and mid-career conversions tied to real posts.

Finally, neither wages nor skills can be fully enhanced in the absence of coherent labour-market planning throughout the economy. And in turn, the requirements for the appropriate management of both wages and skills can be met only through the introduction of sectoral collective bargaining, an essential prerequisite for economic renewal.

9.3 Migration and workers' rights

The migration component of the plan is modest. We estimate about fifteen thousand skilled industrial workers a year would be needed for a pro-labour strategy of reindustrialisation that is designed to complement domestic training and conversions. Workers from abroad would be admitted on the basis of need and linked to priority manufacturing occupations. The programme would be targeted, enforceable and fair, as is required by true internationalism from the labour side. Here are some concrete provisions:

- Equal pay for equal work; full access to union membership and representation under existing law; and clear routes to settlement for those in priority occupations, so firms invest in skills rather than churn staff.
- No recruitment fees for workers; licensing and enforcement against fee-charging, with resourcing to match the task.
- Employers must meet or exceed published going rates and salary thresholds; prohibited costs (such as the Immigration Skills Charge and Certificates of Sponsorship) should not be passed to workers.
- Every sponsored worker in priority sectors is enrolled in employer-backed skill improvement programmes, with public co-funding conditional on apprenticeship places for domestic recruits.
- Remove the No Recourse to Public Funds condition for workers from abroad to ensure access to fundamental

welfare support; in return, require tax compliance and participation in training.

- Health and safety enforcement and labour-market policing must be visible; inspections should be coordinated and intelligence-led.

This is how a reasonable, purpose-built immigration stream would support a domestic rebuilding of skills and jobs, rather than substituting for it. If such immigration was integrated with structures of sectoral collective bargaining throughout the economy, it would help achieve managed growth, fund training, protect standards, and lock in union voice. It would be the opposite of the current model – cheap labour as a crutch for weak investment. And it would sit alongside a national labour plan that would raise pay, expand capacity in technical education, and redeploy workers displaced by technological change.

Step 2. Public ownership

A credible reindustrialisation strategy would use nationalisation and regulatory tools from the perspective of labour – giving them teeth to shift the economic and social balance and restoring a spirit of public service. Ownership and regulation will be organised so that the increase in manufacturing and the rise of GDP translate into benefits for everybody rather than perpetuating a model that benefits a small elite.

Public finance will come with property rights and control. The model of 'de-risking' activities while relying on 'clever' regulation presumably to get socially desired results – characteristic of neoliberalism – has delivered private profits backed by public money and thin results for production. Britain must break with that approach. Public finance ought to come with property rights and control, including equity, voting rights, board seats, trade union representation, and active public management.

Public funds will not be used to tackle the debts of private operators, and prices will not be determined by earnings and replacement costs.

9.4 Immediate public ownership

Three cases justify immediate public ownership. First, natural monopolies, such as high-voltage electricity and high-pressure gas networks, that everyone must use. Public ownership decides who connects, when, and on what terms, and prevents rent extraction. Second, chokepoints, such as a single plant or system feeding many chains (a pipeline, a smelter, a region's last cement kiln). Public ownership guarantees access at reasonable prices. Third, operations that support and ensure skills and certification, for instance, an essential medicines line or a final-assembly hall, where closure would destroy trained workforces and accumulated know-how.

Passenger rail would move to in-house operation as contracts end to avoid committing public funds unnecessarily, so traction, crews and electrification align with production schedules. Buying the rolling-stock leasing companies is probably not necessary at the start because it would involve large sums of money to be paid for financial vehicles whose assets are locked into long leases and regulated returns. The benefits of public control in the first instance could be obtained through regulation, franchise terms, and public procurement. Moreover, only about forty per cent of rail routes are electrified, which underlines the coordination gap that arises as infrastructure is currently planned and funded by one set of actors, fleets are specified and financed by another, operations are run by a third, and the Treasury pays the money. Bringing operations in-house closes that gap.

Water privatisation is a text-book example of the drawbacks of selling off natural monopolies. Bills have risen and infrastructure has not been renewed, while the lack of competition and weak regulation has led to excessive profits for shareholders. Water needs major modernisation through public investment that builds new public property rather than buying out existing operators at inflated regulatory values. The state should finance new treatment works, pipe networks, and reservoirs directly as public assets, targeting bottlenecks and areas of industrial expansion first. Existing private operators would continue under tight regulation, but new capacity built to meet reindustrialisation demand would be publicly owned from day one. Periodic reviews already authorise large programmes through the regulated capital base; targeted project finance with clear public controls manages risk without wholesale nationalisation from the start. The scale of modernisation would be the pathway to fuller public property as assets are renewed.

Beyond utilities, foundational manufacturing also warrants a concrete start of nationalisation. It is important to have public property over actual productive assets that matter for the broader rebuilding of manufacturing. Stressed core steel plants and mills are vital, as is the only remaining aluminium smelter/casting line at Lochaber, and chokepoints in chemicals and plastics. This capacity would act as an anchor for the rebuilding of machinery and other areas.

There is also a case for public ownership in industries that are vital for other parts of manufacturing to thrive. For example, two or three machine-tool firms providing spares, rebuilds and apprenticeships would stabilise maintenance cycles across industry at modest cost. In the advanced sector, finally, public property in the first instance would be reserved for unique platforms at risk of disappearance. Targeted public stakes would ensure the long-term survival of such national assets.

9.5 Public money buys public rights

Unlike many other countries, Britain lacks a fully-fledged economics ministry with the power to get things done. The Treasury's stranglehold over policy needs to be broken and a successor to the National Economic Development Council – abolished by Thatcher – should be created. The reason for that is simple: state capacity is fundamental to contemporary advanced economies and shapes their overall conduct and performance. Britain lacks public institutions with necessary commercial, technical and legal competence. These need to be staffed by project directors, grid-connection and consenting teams, cost engineers, contract managers and turnaround specialists, who would not merely regulate but actively sustain delivery of results at pace.

The initial cost of the nationalisation programme would be modest. Targeted acquisitions and network stakes would probably cost £13 to 19 billion in 2024–5 prices. This sum excludes the large costs of rebuilding and expanding productive capacity together with decarbonisation, which will require a wave of public and private investment, discussed in Step 3. That will be the main lever for creating public property over time.

The reason for state ownership is that public money must buy public rights. Thus, equity co-investment would accompany major grants and connection funding; convertible instruments would turn into voting stakes, if delivery lags; minority stakes at first instance would move to control at network and chokepoints. By applying this fundamental rule, the wave of public investment would help rebuild wealth creation and, stage by stage, accumulate a stock of public property commensurate with public risk. There will be no de-risking of private enterprises.

Finally, public property by itself is no panacea. The real test would be how it is run and in whose favour. It requires a form of governance that treats management as a delegated function of social purpose rather than a semi-sovereign profit centre, so there will be trade union representatives on boards accompanied by public appointees chosen for their technical and commercial competence. Remuneration will be fair but capped at a reasonable multiple of the median wage. Performance will be judged by whether assets deliver reliable output at a competitive unit cost while maintaining safety and skills.

There is ample practical industrial knowledge of how to create adequate tests for this purpose, which would be enforced through independent auditing and oversight by Parliament. The point is to align managerial authority with the interests and rights of labour and of the users of the output. There is ample experience, for instance in Norway's publicly owned electricity grid and Singapore's public transport system, in how to operate in such a manner. It is perfectly possible to subordinate industrial behaviour to public purpose without sacrificing efficiency.

Step 3. An investment wave

9.6 Capital investment in manufacturing

Decades of under-investment will need to be reversed if industrial renaissance is to become a reality. The make-do-and-mend approach has to be replaced by a major capital programme that both renews existing equipment and expands capacity.

We use a simple method to estimate the capital required to hit our target.[1] In 2023, the net manufacturing capital stock of Britain (at current replacement cost) was £292 billion, and the output of manufacturing (in GVA, Gross Value Added) was £223 billion. This makes for a ratio of capital stock to output of 1.31, and this is the figure that

[1] For those with technical training, the method is based on the Harrod–Domar assumption of constant capital intensity; the implied model is stock–flow consistent.

shows the 'capital intensity' of British manufacturing. We assume this ratio remains unchanged over the period. We also assume that fixed capital in manufacturing will continue to depreciate at its current rate of thirteen per cent a year – or £38 billion in today's money.

One more step is needed to work out the required aggregate investment.[2] If the growth of GDP is 2.75 per cent per year (from the base of 2023), then British GDP in 2035 will be £3,842 billion (base year is 2023). With eleven per cent share of manufacturing, the level of manufacturing output will be £423 billion, representing an increase of £195 billion over the period. Since the ratio of capital stock to output is assumed to be constant at 1.31, the capital stock of Britain will have to rise by £255 billion. This gives us the required net investment until 2035. To this sum we must add the investment needed to make good the depreciation of the capital stock until 2035. At a constant depreciation rate of thirteen per cent, the replacement investment over the period would be £545 billion. The gross investment that is required over the period is £800 billion – a large but reasonable figure given the current state of British economy. It should not be seen as a hard target but as a way of assessing the feasibility of reindustrialisation.

It is also important to note that the increase in the capital stock by 2035 would be proportionately much larger than the increase in the labour force that we estimated in Step 1. The manufacturing capital stock rises from £292 billion in 2023 to £547 billion in 2035, but the manufacturing labour force rises from 2.6 million to about 3.3 million. Consequently, the ratio of capital to labour in British manufacturing goes up from £112,000/worker to £166,000/worker.

---

[2] We do not show the arithmetic, to keep the text easy to read. Figures are in 2024–5 prices; 2023 stocks are rebased accordingly. All projections are illustrative, anchored to the latest comprehensive ONS data for 2023. Calculations use K/Y = 1.31 and CFC/Net K ≈ 13% applied to the average net stock.

This represents a substantial rise in 'capital deepening' – more capital per worker. It is a key driver of productivity increase and fully in line with the effort to rebuild the wealth creating potential of the British economy. If Britain wants wages and productivity to rise without mass lay-offs, it must put more – and better – capital behind each worker.

9.7 Key utilities and transport

Britain's investment needs don't end there. The planned manufacturing expansion needs major improvements in the sinews of the economy: water, energy networks, rail and roads. Using official sources, we can form reasonable estimates for these, all based on prices for 2024–5.

For water, the infrastructure needs are massive after years of neglect. A central ten-year estimate for renewal investment would be about £155 billion. For electricity, to reach a clean power system by the mid-2030s compatible with Net Zero, the country should probably be planning for about £340 billion over ten years. This breaks down into roughly £140 billion for new renewables (offshore wind, onshore wind, solar) using the Department for Energy Security and Net Zero's generation-cost benchmarks; about £70 billion for storage; and about £130 billion for grid upgrades.

Great British Energy could be the public developer-owner for early and strategic projects but needs more financial firepower if it is to build new capacity both for power generation and storage. Its current capital is only £8.3 billion, which includes the £2.5 billion earmarked for small modular nuclear reactors. A public developer needs the resources to build green field capacity at pace, and that means increasing Great British Energy's capital and ring fencing the sums devoted to renewables.

For rail, the Office of Rail and Road estimated that £43.1 billion is necessary for operations, maintenance and renewals in 2024 to 2029. If we only take renewals (expired track, signalling, electrification assets, etc.) as the relevant part for investment, we can make a central ten-year estimate of about £42 billion.

For roads, a maintenance-first programme – resurfacing, safety, and targeted industrial corridors – has a central ten-year cost of about £71 billion. This lies within current funding patterns for the Strategic Road Network and local roads maintenance, and aligns with the mandate for zero-emission vehicles (eighty per cent of new cars by 2030; one hundred per cent by 2035).

9.8 How much will it cost overall and who will pay for it?

Over ten years, then, we estimate that the reindustrialisation strategy would require about £1.41 trillion: manufacturing £800 billion; water £155 billion; electricity £340 billion; rail £42 billion; roads £71 billion. A workable split would be about three-fifths public and two-fifths private investment. Financing this investment is perfectly possible for the UK as will be shown in the following chapters. What matters at this point is that public money buys public rights. On this basis, the split could work as follows.

On the public side, investment would cover the foundations, such as high-voltage grids and substations, ready-to-build public industrial sites (land assembled and cleaned, roads and drainage, water, sewerage, and power in place), plant connections to various networks, labour skills, and so on. It would build new plants where none exist. In those cases, public investment would build and own the site and the plant from day one. These funds would come with shares, voting control, and trade union representation.

On the private side, firms would finance specific equipment lines, build generation units feeding into public grids under fixed-price contracts, and create storage installations with capped returns. Critically, private investment in manufacturing will occur primarily as lessors or contractors to public facilities in foundational and enabling sectors, not as owners of the productive base. In advanced manufacturing where flexibility matters, private ownership can be strongly present, but only after foundational capacity is publicly controlled and union density is established across supply chains aided by the statutory establishment of mechanisms of collective bargaining. Business risk stays with private firms, but they operate within a framework that is fundamentally determined by public ownership and control.

Attracting private investment would require a clear plan and firm commitments by the public sector, not socialising business risk as is currently the case. A programme for renewables, storage and grids could come with fixed connection dates. Standard long contracts would make cash flows easy to understand. Training places for workers from Step 1 would be written into contracts so projects start on time. Where private capital would not move first, for instance, early steel units, new chemicals lines, strategic components, public build-and-own would put the first capacity on the ground for others to plug into. These are all significant advantages for private enterprises that accept the basic framework: fixed contracts, capped returns, equipment supply in return for compatibility standards, trade union representation, and training commitments.

The sequencing of the investment plan matters. Public investment that builds and owns the assets establishes foundational capacity in steel, chemicals, machine tools and strategic components, thus creating an anchor for private investment downstream. This reverses the current model where the state de-risks and private capital extracts. Private capital enters where its flexibility potentially benefits production, not where its ownership would concentrate power over employment decisions, automation deployment, or wage determination in critical industries.

Britain's climate change targets are ambitious, and the proposed investment wave is a practical route to meeting them while rebuilding industry. The lever for delivering it is the programme itself, run by the fundamental rule. Public equity would accompany major grants and connections; loans would turn into shares if delivery lagged; public stakes would increase to control single assets that set the terms for many others.

And where needed, new plants would be built and kept in public hands. Public ownership in new foundational capacity ensures that decisions are made by institutions with trade union representation on boards, not by firms maximising shareholder returns. Step by step, the investment wave would finance the assets the economy needs and build a stock of public property that matches the scale of public risk.

A final word of caution is necessary: the investment plan is coherent and adds up, but it is tight. It assumes gains in growth and productivity, timely grid connections, a step-up in training and a state with both the capacity and the mindset to foster change. Turning it into policy would require further detailed work and a clear assessment of risks. It is not a detailed blueprint but a roadmap to structure the debate while also being fit for use.

10
Finance, trade and capital flows

Step 4. A public bank

10.1 Rebalancing public and private finance

There is no escaping the fact that the investment programme is large and that financing it would be a major concern. The financing task could be split into two parts: fund the public share at low, stable cost; and organise finance so that private capital follows at scale but without extracting rents from projects shaped by public policy. Key to meeting these tasks would be the establishment of a purpose-built Public Investment Bank (PIB) with real balance-sheet strength and operating under the fundamental rule: public money buys public rights.

Britain needs a well-capitalised PIB to provide long-term and predictable finance. This could emerge from the UK Infrastructure Bank, which was launched in June 2021 and was consolidated into the National Wealth Fund from October 2024. Its legal objectives are to support the transition to Net Zero and regional and local growth. This follows international practice, for instance, Germany's public development bank Kreditanstalt für Wiederaufbau

(KfW) and the EU's European Investment Bank (EIB) typically engage in patient lending to crowd in private capital and deliver key pieces of infrastructure.

The general case for a PIB is simple. Long-term industrial projects spend heavily upfront – on planning and design, site works and foundations, and network connections – while revenue arrives only after commissioning. Private lenders charge higher interest rates than a public bank, which can hold its charges low to match policy aims.

The availability of long-term credit in the British financial system is limited despite the great expansion of the financial sector during the last four decades. A PIB makes long-term loans at lower cost, which it would patiently hold through all development stages.

Reindustrialisation on the scale proposed by our strategy is not credible without a PIB. The investment funding needed is too large and the maturities are too long for private markets to deliver at an acceptable cost. A PIB supplies long-duration, programmatic credit, sets reference prices that compress interest rate spreads, and co-lends with pension funds and insurance institutions to get assets built. It also gives the strategy a public character by attaching ownership and control to public capital. In doing so, it curbs the City of London's structural power over investment and marks a clear break with the neoliberal settlement.

10.2 A powerful public bank at last

To deliver the programme, the PIB must be sufficiently capitalised, with a paid-in equity base of about £60 billion, phased over four years. It would be considerably larger than the National Wealth Fund's current £27.8 billion of committed capacity but still proportionate to the task and within Britain's means. With initial leverage around four times the size of equity, perhaps rising to five or six times subject to performance, the bank could carry roughly £240 billion of loans and guarantees and, by recycling repayments and co-lending with pension funds and insurers, could push cumulative support above £300 billion over the decade.

The PIB will operate under the governance principles established for public ownership in Step 2. Its board will include appointed representatives from unions in sectors receiving finance, and public appointees chosen for commercial and technical competence rather than political connections. Board remuneration will be capped at a reasonable multiple of the median wage of PIB employees. Lending decisions will be made against published criteria, such as alignment with reindustrialisation priorities, labour standards compliance, apprenticeship commitments, and financial viability. There will be independent audit of loan performance and annual reporting to Parliament on deployment by sector, default rates, and job creation. This governance structure ensures efficiency and prevents the PIB from becoming another captured institution serving private finance under public branding.

The balance sheet would be kept simple, with no 'exotic' financial instruments that invite speculation. On the asset side, there would be long-term loans in sterling to build factories, depots and the connections they need (power, water, grid, road, rail). The loans could be structured to encourage pension funds and insurers to participate by allocating more of the risk towards the PIB. There will also be straightforward completion and availability guarantees, with penalties if deadlines are missed or performance falls short. On the liability side, there will be equity paid in by the government and plain sterling bonds issued at rates close to gilts. The PIB will further rely on recycled funds as the loans it makes are repaid.

10.3 Insurer and pension fund firepower harnessed

Important as the PIB would be, the real firepower within the British financial system lies with insurance companies and pension funds, which hold a large share of the country's savings. Occupational pension schemes held about £2.05 trillion of assets at end-September 2024, with the assets of insurers also around the £2 trillion mark. Diverting eight to twelve per cent of these vast pools of money towards long-term UK assets amounts from £320 to £470 billion. Even if only a portion proved to be investable, the sums would still be large.

Voluntary reallocation of these funds through the goodwill of the institutions or from their plain search for profits is highly unlikely at this scale. Government intervention will be needed for savings to go where the country needs them. There is plenty of choice: set legal minimum shares for public pension schemes that rise towards ten per cent in qualifying British productive assets, with a simple charge on funds that fall short and a rebate for those that comply; require default workplace pensions to hold a 'productive UK' slice via plain pooled funds that lend to long-term domestic projects with predictable repayments. These should be binding regulations.

To be more precise, insurers should receive licences, and pension defaults should be approved, only on condition that they hold a statutory minimum of qualifying British productive assets. The collective savings of the British people must be turned into plant, kit, and connections rather than being fed into the City of London's fast circuits of global money capital; failure to meet the floor would trigger automatic penalties and a freeze on discretionary permissions until compliance is restored.

Such measures would move control away from the City towards those involved in production. Any project taking public money, such as grants, connections, guarantees, and land, would route its debt through the PIB as lender, co-lender, or pricing anchor; the PIB would publish a standing price and standard documents, and private lenders would either match or step aside. The result is that the public becomes the price-maker in long-dated sterling loans, domestic savings are anchored in productive assets, and finance is tied to delivery and public rights. That would be an important shift towards the economic policy change that Britain needs.

Step 5. Regulating trade

10.4 Trade regulation is necessary

Britain likes to think of itself as an advanced country and in many respects that's true. Living standards, despite the stagnation of the past decade and a half, are high by global standards. Yet when it comes to trade policy, Britain needs to think of itself as a developing country that is seeking to protect its fledgling industries from the full force of international competition. Any industrial strategy will be stillborn unless the new capacity has the time to put down strong roots. Left to an unqualified free-trade stance, UK producers would be routinely undercut by imports built on lower wages, laxer labour and safety enforcement, cheaper carbon, subsidised power and credit, export rebates, currency management, tax holidays and state-sponsored capacity.

A determined reindustrialisation strategy must therefore align trade policy with domestic investment and employment. There is no shame in this. Just as trade controls are normally required to allow a new industrialiser to enter the world market, they are also required to allow a re-industrialiser to rebuild necessary productive capacity. Controlling trade is a regular instrument of economic policy, like taxation, competition law or monetary policy; it should be used to defend productive industry, good jobs and external balance. Transforming the lopsided and dysfunctional UK economy is not possible otherwise.

10.5 The tools are already available – with help from carbon

Faced with this imperative, the UK already has available to it a set of possible measures that could be deployed to form a new policy of trade control in line with its reindustrialisation strategy.

The World Trade Organization is a pillar of the neoliberal Washington Consensus that sets the baseline for global trade: non-discrimination, transparency, and respect for tariff ceilings. But it allows targeted measures, such as anti-dumping, countervailing duties and safeguards, when there is evidence of harm. It also recognises exceptions for the environment, public morals and security, if measures are even-handed and necessary. Similarly, the Agreement on Government Procurement opens covered public contracts among its parties on equal terms and permits performance-based criteria (for example, carbon limits and reliability) so long as they apply equally to domestic and foreign bidders and do not disguise nationality tests.

Moreover, from 2027 a Carbon Border Adjustment Mechanism (CBAM) adopted by the UK would equalise the carbon price of imports in iron and steel, aluminium, cement, fertilisers and hydrogen. The remedies permitted under WTO rules are already provided for in UK law, with the steel safeguard being a live precedent.

The Procurement Act 2023 would allow contracting authorities to award contracts on the basis of their long-term costs, embodied carbon, reliability and delivery risk, provided the criteria are outcome-based, transparent and non-discriminatory. In practice, model tenders would require audited supply-chain traceability and labour-law compliance; proven reliability; delivery plans; open-book pricing with caps on advisory fees; step-in rights where public money is at risk; and training and apprenticeship commitments. Product and process standards – covering carbon disclosure, labour compliance, safety and traceability – would be tightened and enforced at the border.

Taken together, these instruments could function as standing, rules-based controls on trade that support reindustrialisation. The aim of the policy would be simple: secure demand, keep new plants busy, lower unit costs, and stop import surges from hollowing out capacity.

10.6 And could be made still harder

If Britain decided, or was forced, truly to prioritise domestic industry over multilateral niceties, there are firmer tools to hand for trade regulation. The United States under Donald Trump's second administration has already normalised unilateral tariffs, national-security trade actions and broad, managed-trade deals. The environment of global trade is no longer rules-first but power-first.

In that world, the UK could set reciprocal import quotas or tariff-rate quotas in critical inputs; apply surcharges where persistent distortions are evident; run anti-circumvention rules to stop trans-shipment, that is, the practice of routing goods through third countries to disguise their true origin and evade tariffs, quotas or other trade restrictions; make national security determinations for core supply chains and require import licences, local testing and audit rights; attach domestic content conditions to public subsidies, permits and grid connections in strategic sectors; screen outbound investment so UK capital and technology do not build foreign capacity that undercuts domestic plant; and deploy export controls where leverage exists.

The escalation to harder measures would be triggered by clear thresholds, such as import surges in strategic sectors; persistent dumping margins despite remedies; documented cases of overcapacity targeting UK markets; or evidence that trading partners are systematically blocking UK exports while flooding UK markets. Where triggers are met, government would first deploy tariff-rate quotas with transparent caps, then escalate to quantitative restrictions or domestic-content requirements if dumping persists. The escalation ladder would be a matter of agreed public policy under Parliament oversight.

Clearly, such measures carry significant risks. Britain should expect retaliation and plan for it: a clear escalation ladder, market-diversification support for exposed exporters, targeted export-credit backing, and strategic stockpiles for critical inputs. But some elements of such a mechanism are already in place, for instance, in the UK steel safeguard.

Free-trade orthodoxy has contributed to a lopsided economy and weak productivity. A credible reindustrialisation strategy would pair domestic investment with trade and the rule that public money buys public rights. Controlling trade is a core function of economic policy. Used consistently, it would protect wages and productive capacity and restore balance to Britain's transactions with the rest of the world.

Step 6. Capital controls and a change of course for Britain

10.7 The imperative of capital controls

Capital controls are easily the most controversial aspect of the reindustrialisation strategy. Britain has been strongly committed to free capital flows since 1979, which is hardly surprising for a country that is home to the City of London and one of the most financialised economies in the world. In British public debate the notion of adopting capital controls is akin to heresy.

Yet capital controls are widely used across the world, including in developed countries. Indeed, even the IMF, another pillar of the Washington Consensus, has gradually acknowledged that capital controls could be a legitimate economic policy where systemic risk is present, if measures are targeted, transparent and time-bounded. The OECD Code of Liberalisation also allows for temporary derogations from free capital movement with notification and review. In truth, capital controls have always been a legitimate component of economic policy and Britain used to have a wide array of such controls from the end of the Second World War to the late 1970s.

Reindustrialisation on the scale set out in our strategy is not risk free: imports of equipment and materials arrive early, while export capacity and productivity gains arrive later. The programme is large – about £1.41 trillion over ten years, of which roughly three-fifths is public investment – and the bulk of capacity building would perhaps take four years to complete.

If capital was left entirely frictionless and uncontrolled, market interest rates and gilt yields would be shaped by speculative trading by mobile money capital. That would be amplified by the structural weaknesses of the British economy: a persistent current account deficit of roughly three per cent of GDP, foreign holdings of government debt of more than thirty per cent, and the UK banks' vast stock of external liabilities of close to $6 trillion at the end of 2024.

Capital controls are therefore not an optional extra; they are part of the normal policy kit that will be necessary to protect domestic investment, jobs and the external position of Britain. The broad case was substantively made in Chapter 7. The need for controls was further discussed in Step 4 of this chapter, which argued for directing insurers and pensions, which together manage about £4 trillion, towards long-term UK assets.

10.8 Some commonsense measures

Capital controls can change the price and timing of fast-moving money. The state armoury is replete with possible measures to achieve that. Already in Chapter 8 we discussed Tobin taxes on very short-term trades raising the cost of pure speculation without touching long-term investors. Along similar lines, a small, time-limited cash deposit at the central bank for very short inflows makes quick roundtrips of money capital less profitable; short minimum holding periods and onshore clearing for key contracts also slow the churn of money capital.

The economics of such controls is simple: make money capital go towards longer-term investments so interest rates and the exchange rate move less violently. It is important to note that financial regulators across the world already back some of the basic thinking of these controls. Thus, investment funds that let people take money out daily are expected or recommended to make those who leave pay for the trading costs their exit causes as well as set withdrawal terms that match how quickly the fund can sell what it owns. Even international regulators, such as the Financial Stability Board, are amenable to some elements of this approach, for instance, concerning the guidance to manage liquidity by investment funds.

Other, more serious, controls can make balance sheets safer and steer savings into real investment. Banks, for instance, could be stopped from relying heavily on short-term foreign funding or taking large one-way currency bets. Limits on both lower the chances that a major financial crisis would emerge. Furthermore, borrowers who earn revenue in pounds but borrow in foreign currency should face tighter standards because unexpected exchange-rate moves can destroy them. These proposals are in line with the previously mentioned measure of channelling a share of pension and insurance assets towards long-term UK investment projects. They are now widely accepted ideas on how to manage capital flows.

10.9 Harsher measures also available, if needed

There are, however, even harder measures that should be kept in reserve. The list is long: stronger rules could be imposed on domestic borrowers who borrow in foreign currency but earn revenues in sterling and thus run substantial risks from sudden exchange rate fluctuations; exporters could be required to convert foreign exchange within a certain deadline; cash deposit requirements could be imposed on short-term inflows of money capital.

The aim of controls is not to micromanage the international flows of money capital, nor to stop them altogether. It is to prevent money capital from disrupting the functioning of the productive sector of the economy and to limit the power of finance over economic policy. These aims and some of the measures that make them possible are widely adopted across the world and even by some of the major economies, such as China and India.

10.10 Expect fierce opposition

Whatever options the British government adopts, it could expect the City of London to oppose capital controls loudly and in concert. For one thing, finance will argue that it makes a large contribution to public revenue. For 2023/24, HMRC records £24.9 billion in PAYE and NICs from banking employees and £9.3 bn in corporation tax from banks, plus £1.4 billion from the bank levy and £1.5 billion from the bank surcharge, making a total of £37.1 billion. Furthermore, there was a trade surplus from financial services of £73.2 billion in 2023.

These sums are large but the bulk of PAYE and NICs mostly reflects high pay in the financial sector since it is largely taxes collected from employees. It is not some kind of a unique contribution that should immunise the sector from targeted measures to reduce hot-money volatility. As for the corporation tax, that also reflects the increase in the rate to twenty-five per cent in 2023, not the underlying profitability. The significance of the tax sums is typically exaggerated to protect the interests of finance.

The City of London will also argue that even light restraints on fast-moving cross-border money capital would raise borrowing costs, push business to other financial centres, and weaken the UK's standing in the world economy. In parallel, it will press for exceptions and long grace periods, threaten legal action, redesign products to sidestep rules, and create pressure in the bond and the foreign currency markets to force concessions. The reindustrialisation strategy is, after all, a clash of models: the City's privileged position in financialised capitalism rests on speed and scale of short-term money capital flows; policies that change the price or timing of those flows will face organised resistance.

Adopting capital controls represents a regime break that is necessary for reindustrialisation, but it certainly does not signal a retreat from the world. The proposal restricts very short-term financial speculation, raises the weight of patient domestic capital in long-dated productive assets, and ties public investment to building plants and producing output. Finance would be a pillar supporting production, not a predatory presence on it.

Capital controls must be sensible and plainly justified; they should be targeted and transparent in terms of purpose and the events that would trigger their use; they should also be aligned with monetary and fiscal policy as well as being constantly monitored for market effects and unintended consequences, leading to quick adjustment. The international rulebook already accepts the idea of targeted measures. London's legal infrastructure, depth, and financial networks will not evaporate because the government will introduce targeted and transparent controls, and that is why carefully designed measures are unlikely to trigger wholesale flight. The City will complain ferociously and then it will find new ways to operate.

11
Can we afford it?

11.1 The ogre of public debt

Liz Truss had the shortest tenure as prime minister in Britain's history, lasting only seven weeks in Downing Street in the autumn of 2022 as her time in office quickly descended into chaos. But, while Truss has become synonymous with political ineptitude, in two respects she was right. Britain in the fourteen years of Conservative rule had been caught in a low-growth, high-debt trap. Moreover, there could be no escape from that trap while the forces of orthodoxy – the Bank of England, the Treasury, the Office for Budget Responsibility, and think tanks like the Institute for Fiscal Studies – maintained their vice-like grip on what is and what is not possible or affordable.

It is worth stressing that ours is not a business-as-usual approach. The industrialisation strategy will have major implications for the public finances, but also for monetary policy and the role of the Bank of England. We are explicit about regime change: Britain cannot drift back to the settlement that produced stagnation. The purpose is to rebuild the country's capacity to create wealth; fiscal and monetary policy will be aligned to that end. The strategy will be bold but careful – not conservative – and public finances will have to make it possible.

The public finance problem that the UK currently faces is straightforward, as we showed in the earlier chapters. After more than four decades of managing public spending, taxes, and borrowing on neoliberal principles, including repeated austerity, the government's share of aggregate demand in 2025 is larger than in the late 1970s, while it has under-invested in productive capacity and infrastructure, as was shown in chapter 4. It also runs persistent fiscal deficits and has a large public debt.

This predicament is the direct result of weak wealth creation to which the state has contributed through under-investment. The task now is to shift policy towards rebuilding wealth creation through power, grids, transport corridors, ready-to-build sites, skills and foundational industry, while containing short-run fiscal and monetary risks. Public debt should be assessed in that context.

The first and crucial step is to reject the hidebound Treasury View that considers public investment dispensable and puts priority on controlling current government expenditure in the hope of keeping headline public borrowing under control. Public debt is not a problem if it supports boosting productive capacity.

If capacity expands and generates returns, public borrowing creates the means of its own repayment. Currently the national debt is mostly serviced in the bond markets, and so the financial system commands power over public policy. Government borrows from private investors who essentially set the rates of interest the state should pay and then invests the payments from the public purse in private speculation. A public bank with capital controls and the Bank of England as active supporter can break this pattern and subordinate finance to production.

11.2 We can afford it

The strategy will certainly require an increase in public debt because – as was shown in chapter 9 – our re-industrialisation plan calls for total investment of about £1.41 trillion over ten years. The public share would be roughly three-fifths, or about £850 billion, averaging £85 billion a year. The sum is large but its impact on the public finances can be managed to avoid major disturbance. A plausible approach over the decade would be to split it into £365 billion to build grids, sites, rail and water renewals, and early plant. The remaining £485 billion would be invested in earning assets held by the public, such as long-dated loans and equity originated by the PIB and by utilities with regulated cash flows. Markets observe gross debt, but solvency and sustainability depend on growth and on the income-generating assets that stand behind that debt. Borrowing to build assets that yield cash flow and raise productive capacity is fundamentally different from borrowing to cover current consumption. The relevant measure of exposure is therefore the state's net financial position over time, not a headline borrowing figure taken in isolation.

11.3 A new national account sheet

The government could raise the extra funding mainly by selling more long-term bonds as well as by issuing green bonds, where they clearly cut borrowing costs, as well as lifting National Savings targets so households help fund the programme. It could make the domestic demand for bonds more reliable by setting clear rules for pension funds and insurers to hold more long-term UK bonds and Public Investment Bank bonds tied to real projects, and by publishing a regular calendar of bond sales. The Debt Management Office and the Public Investment Bank would coordinate their sale calendars. Monetary policy will be aligned with the investment strategy. During the build phase, the Bank of England would avoid shrinking its gilt holdings in ways that destabilise issuance, reinvesting maturities and, if necessary, smoothing bond markets to ensure orderly financing conditions. This would not suspend monetary discipline; it would recognise that a coordinated macroeconomic strategy requires fiscal and monetary authorities to act in concert.

Funding will be facilitated by keeping public loans and equity on strict economic terms. That means that the government will charge interest or take dividends, demand security where sensible, and would not slip grants in by the back door. Prices will be set by independent valuation, and the terms will be simple. The assets will be plain, without clever off-balance-sheet tricks.

Each year the government will publish a short schedule that shows three things: gross debt and borrowing; the stock of financial assets and the income they earn; and the state's net worth. Guarantees and backstops will never be free. The government will charge a fee, set a loss provision in the budget, and set a cap on the liability. If a project needs more than that, it will be redesigned or rejected. There will be no free lunches.

Bond markets respond to credibility, growth prospects and refinancing risk. A programme that lengthens maturities, builds domestic institutional demand, generates asset income and raises long-term growth strengthens that credibility. Gross issuance matters, but what ultimately anchors borrowing costs is the economy's capacity to grow and to generate reliable cash flows.

The programme does not require immediate and across the board tax increases. As productive capacity comes on stream and revenue rises, the primary balance can move steadily towards balance. If conditions tighten unexpectedly, targeted revenue measures remain available, but the strategy does not depend on front-loaded tax hikes to be credible.

If conditions tighten – interest rates run above nominal growth and foreign demand for bonds weakens – the government will slow new starts, put more money into assets that pay sooner, and use targeted revenue to hold the primary balance.

11.4 The Bank of England

Monetary policy will actively support the strategy for reindustrialisation, as was already mentioned in the previous section. Central bank 'independence' is a shibboleth of the neoliberal era whose time has passed. The Bank of England is a public institution, and part of its mission should be to use its control over the nation's credit money to help rebuild the nation's productive base. It must back the investment wave and not simply focus on keeping inflation low.

The short-term jump in inflation in the 2020s came primarily from supply weaknesses not from excess aggregate demand due to consumption. The priority for Britain is to add productive capacity; as new power, grids, sites and plant would come online, inflationary pressures will ease.

The Bank of England should stand ready to finance a measured share of public investment. It has already created vast amounts of money to fund state spending since 2007–9 and again in 2020–1. Moreover, and as was already shown in chapter 4, there are substantial flows of public money from the Treasury to the Bank as its bond holdings are run down. There is no case for the Bank continuing with its hurried balance-sheet shrinkage. Forced public bond sales push up funding costs and crystallise losses that the Treasury then indemnifies. The Bank should be holding rather than selling its gilt stock, reinvesting maturities, and, if needed, buying in the market to smooth issuance of new bonds. At the same time, it should be keeping interest rates low, predictable, and as stable as possible while the building of new capacity is under way.

Both fiscal and monetary policy can be creatively and feasibly deployed to help bring to fruition the reindustrialisation plan, while keeping public debt within manageable bounds. The core rule stands: public money buys public rights. Britain borrows to build productive capacity that lifts wages, output and the state's own revenues. The government publishes the path and manages the funding. With boldness and determination, the country will turn the corner. As we show in the concluding chapters, stronger wealth creation will be good for workers, good for communities and good for the planet.

Box 11.1 The bond markets

Myth of Invincibility and How to Contain Them

When politicians warn that the bond markets will not allow a policy, they mean that financial investors may demand higher interest rates to hold government debt, making borrowing more expensive. Higher yields can raise mortgage costs, put pressure on the exchange rate, and fuel inflation narratives. This is presented as a natural market reaction, but it is mostly a political constraint enforced through financial institutions.

Bond markets matter because modern states roll over large volumes of debt continuously. If yields spike, governments face pressure to change course unless they control the central bank and are willing to use it. That vulnerability is not inevitable but political.

A government pursuing economic transformation has three crucial lines of action available to it.

First, the central bank can act as lender of last resort to the state itself, not only to banks. A government that issues debt in its own currency and controls its central bank cannot be forced into default by bond market pressure. The Bank of England can stabilise gilt markets through purchases, repo operations, and collateral rules whenever the Treasury authorises it. This was done during the 2008 financial crisis, when the Bank bought £375 billion of gilts through quantitative easing, and again during the pandemic. The constraint is political will, not technical capacity. If the central bank refuses to act, it is because it has been granted operational independence that allows it to block transformative fiscal policy.

The Public Investment Bank proposed in this book operates in close coordination with the Bank of England to break the City of London's control over long-term industrial finance. The PIB issues bonds to fund productive investment in manufacturing, energy, and infrastructure. These bonds are made eligible, by mandate, as collateral at the Bank of England on transparent terms, allowing the Bank to provide liquidity against them. This creates a reference rate for long-dated sterling credit tied to productive assets rather than speculative returns.

When pension funds and insurance companies are required to hold a statutory minimum of PIB paper and other qualifying productive assets, as this book proposes, the market for long-term finance is fundamentally restructured. The state becomes the price-maker for patient capital, not the price-taker. Commercial lenders must either match PIB terms or step aside. This removes a key mechanism through which financial markets have constrained industrial policy, namely the ability to price long-term credit beyond what productive investment can bear.

Second, capital controls can close the channels through which speculative pressure operates. Capital flight is not a natural phenomenon but a set of transactions, such as short-term portfolio outflows, wholesale funding withdrawals, derivatives positioning, and corporate balance-sheet shifts. Each of these can be monitored, taxed, delayed, or restricted. Controls need not be permanent or comprehensive to be effective.

Crucially, destabilising pressure does not arise only from capital leaving an economy. Short-term capital inflows can be equally disruptive, inflating asset prices, leading to exchange rate appreciation, and encouraging balance-sheet structures that become fragile when conditions change. For this reason, many capital control regimes focus on inflows as well as outflows, using instruments such as reserve requirements on portfolio inflows, minimum holding periods, taxes on short-term investments and limits on foreign currency borrowing. These measures are designed to discourage speculative finance, while permitting trade credit and long-term productive investment.

Malaysia during the 1997–8 Asian crisis imposed selective controls that addressed both exit and entry channels. The government restricted offshore trading of the ringgit, the Malaysian currency; required approval for certain portfolio movements; and introduced time-based measures that penalised short-term capital while allowing longer-term investment. Capital that had fled returned within months, the economy stabilised, and controls were later relaxed. Recovery was faster than in neighbouring countries that followed IMF-led liberalisation programmes.

Chile in the 1990s used an unremunerated reserve requirement on capital inflows, requiring investors to deposit up to thirty per cent of an inflow with the central bank for a specified period, typically one year, earning no interest. This filtered out short-term speculative capital, while allowing longer-term investment to proceed. The parameters of the scheme were adjusted over time, but the mechanism demonstrably reduced financial volatility without choking productive investment.

China maintains comprehensive capital account restrictions, including approval requirements for both inward and outward investment above set thresholds, limits on foreign currency conversion by residents and tight controls on derivatives activity. These measures have been central to China's ability to pursue industrial policy without being disciplined by speculative capital flows. Iceland after its 2008 banking collapse imposed strict controls on both inflows and outflows, stabilised the currency and dismantled the regime gradually as recovery took hold.

In practice, most developing countries already apply capital controls in tacit or selective form, through administrative approval regimes, differentiated reserve requirements or informal guidance to domestic banks. Since the global financial crisis, even the International Monetary Fund has accepted that 'capital flow management measures' can be legitimate tools for macroeconomic and financial stability under conditions of volatile cross-border flows. The question is therefore not technical feasibility but political willingness to override the preferences of financial markets.

Third, credible delivery of the economic programme itself changes the terrain of policy. Bond markets do not respond mechanically to debt levels but to expectations about growth, inflation and political stability. A government that expands productive capacity, cuts energy costs through public ownership, and builds supply chain resilience creates the material basis for sustained growth while reducing import dependence and inflationary pressure. Markets punish governments that announce ambitious plans without institutional capacity to deliver them. They respond differently when public investment visibly produces results, such as new factories opening, grid connections completed on schedule and training programmes meeting skilled labour requirements.

The power of bond markets is not absolute but conditional on whether governments control monetary institutions, regulate capital flows and demonstrate delivery capacity. Governments that grasp this crucial point can act decisively. Japan has run public debt well above twice GDP for decades without bond market revolt because its central bank acts decisively and its financial system is domestically anchored. Those that treat financial markets as sovereign over elected authority are unable to do so. This is precisely the arrangement neoliberalism was designed to enforce in Britain and elsewhere.

Part III

Making It Happen – Who And How To Do It

12
Rebuilding union power

12.1 Classical liberalism and the assault on labour

Deep in the heart of rural Dorset lies the village of Tolpuddle. It is an unlikely spot to have become a beacon for the struggle for workers' rights, but it was here in 1834 that six farm labourers were arrested, tried and transported to Australia on trumped-up charges for forming a friendly society. The 'crime' of the Tolpuddle Martyrs was to seek to act collectively to resist wage cuts that reduced their already meagre incomes to near-starvation levels.

This was the brutal reality of capitalism during the first incarnation of economic liberalism in the early nineteenth century. Just like neoliberalism, classical liberalism was a political settlement that involved a powerful state delivering for a particular class interest. Just like neoliberalism, classical liberalism was based on certain principles: free movement of goods and money capital, the barest of welfare provision to force people to work, and balanced budgets. And just like neoliberalism, classical liberalism proved unsustainable.

The British trade union movement was the first independent movement of organised workers in the world.

Its growth was integral to the eventual achievement of the universal suffrage at eighteen, which was only fully attained in 1968 when a vote for all at the age of eighteen was introduced. Its political culture was built on a deep class consciousness that all those who worked, regardless of income levels, occupation, race, religion or creed, should be united in one completely non-sectarian movement with one trade union centre. It was power at work that mattered, and this was seen as being the key to wider political and social powers.

While not the only agent for change, it was no co-incidence that the century between 1850 and 1950 saw both the growth of the trade union movement and an improvement in the lot of working people. A welfare state was created, paid for largely by taxing the better off. The Labour Party was founded to represent the working class in parliament. Full employment was adopted as the over-riding aim of economic policy. Above all, the trade union movement grew in size and importance, reaching a peak of more than half the workforce by the late 1970s. Collective bargaining covered more than three-quarters of employees.

It was this settlement that was rolled back from the late 1970s onwards. Central to the success of Thatcherism was the deliberate weakening of the British trade union movement. Union density has fallen to just over one in five workers. Collective bargaining now covers twenty per cent of employees, compared with nearly all workers in France and nearly ninety per cent in Sweden. Yet to this day workers join unions because as organisations they understand the development and defence of their workplace skills and have power over production and standards of work in their trades.

Such powers were not achieved because of their union's political persuasion or favourite church, but because of the combination and organisation of workers. British trade unions have therefore been specialists in their nature, that is committed to the quality of production, skill, technique, expertise and social standing of the work being undertaken as much as the dignity and conditions of their workers. This has been their source of understanding and commitment to the health of the wider economy. Narrowing the role of unions to simply jobs, pay and conditions is misleading.

12.2 Power and success

Most of the 5,400 or so trade unions that have existed in British history have been quite small organisations rising out of particular separate trades. General trade unions, which organise across a variety of industrial sectors and trades, have been the exception, not the rule. General trade unions may sometimes have large memberships, but often they have lacked power across a range of issues relevant to workers in the workplace. Many specialist, largely single occupation, unions, for example those for teachers, nurses, civil servants or communication workers, or historically for engineers or coal miners, have combined strength in understanding the workplace with strength in numbers.

With extensive power and influence, trade unions and community groups scored substantial post-war successes and helped drastically to narrow the divide between the wealthiest and the lowest paid. In the vastly different political and ideological climate of the first post-war decades, the fabric of social life was transformed by full employment with manufacturing at its heart. Political power in the workplace meant wealth was more evenly shared between the boardroom and the shop floor.

The pay gap between men and women also narrowed. The gender-pay-gap pioneer strikers began their dispute for equal pay at Ford in Dagenham in 1968 and the first substantial Equal Pay Act was introduced in 1970. In 1976, despite the implementation of the Equal Pay and Sex Discrimination acts the year before, workers at the Trico-Folberth windscreen-wiper factory in Brentford walked out after the management refused to eliminate the £6 differential between male and female wages. Their ultimate success was a decisive moment in the enforcement of equal pay legislation and reverberates still.

It was also in 1976 that the movement supported the largely female and Asian workforce at Grunwick film-processing factory in their struggle for union recognition. A two-year strike ensued and, despite many complexities and significant setbacks, the struggle expressed a shift in race and gender relations in the country. Racism was confronted by the passing in 1976 of the Race Relations Act, a development that reflected years of struggle by unions.

A vigorous, well-organised and buoyant trade-union movement also meant significant advances in the most basic areas of protection of workers at work. The 1974 Health and Safety at Work Act was internationally pioneering legislation and was emulated in many countries seeking a more progressive settlement for workers. It had the effect within a relatively short space of time of reducing fatalities and serious accidents at work by some eighty per cent.

The post-war growth and strengthening of the independent trade union movement in Britain involved a number of cultural aspects that emboldened and deepened solidarities. There was a strong tradition of political education; many unions had their own education centres and libraries. The study of philosophy, economics, working-class history and organising techniques were deeply embedded in trade union learning.

Adult residential colleges like Coleg Harlech, Ruskin, Northern and others were developed to extend opportunities to learning at the highest levels and help supply future community and trade union leaders. Generations of leaders were systematically trained in ideas, as well as organisational governance and negotiating techniques. Inevitably the popularity of trade unions and the extent of active involvement in their democratic structures meant that there were deep bonds made within the local communities and with community organisations that shared similar values and commitments to improving working-class life. This integration of organisations fighting for the wage at work and the social wage in terms of all other services and facilities needed to foster a more comfortable existence, was an important feature of national life. It followed that if the neoliberal onslaught were to succeed through obeisance to the market and privatisation, this organisational and cultural unity had to be broken ideologically and legislatively.

12.3 De-industrialisation and the erosion of union organisation

The weakening of unions was engineered through two interconnected processes: the shackling of collective action by law and the physical destruction of industrial capacity. Legislative changes transformed the British unions from among the independent to among the most restricted and legislated against and state controlled in the world. This attack was a meticulously planned attack on the heart of union strength: collective solidarity.

The principles and practice of collective solidarity in action both within a union and across unions were universal and deeply held – do not cross a picket line and do not oppose your union's democratically taken decisions. If you did, the union would lawfully discipline you and even expel you. If another group of workers outside your workplace was having a hard time, you would lose pay to strike to support them. Anti-trade union legislation from the early eighties sought to prevent secondary solidarity action and confine this influence to strictly defined boundaries with each employer. Supporting workers outside your workplace with any form of industrial action was criminalised. Until this legal constraint is removed the ability of unions to influence and shape the economy and political direction of the country will be limited.

For generations, British trade unions had been fiercely independent. Of the 128 unions registered with the Certification Officer in 2025 only eleven are affiliated to the Labour Party. And, until the Thatcher legislation of the 1980s, the idea that the state would legislate how unions elected officers or balloted for strikes was anathema. Post-war governments did not dare attempt it until Harold Wilson's abortive In Place of Strife proposals in the late 1960s.

When workers defied pre-Thatcher laws – as with the Pentonville Five in 1972 – mass mobilisation forced their release. By the 1980s, such resistance was ground down. Unions that broke the law faced crippling fines. Individual workers were jailed. The 2024 Employment Rights Bill, despite Labour's landslide victory, left the framework largely intact. The shackles remained.

De-industrialisation dealt heavy blows to the most organised unions. Millions of jobs were lost as whole industries were gutted. The steel strike of 1980 marked the beginning of systematic undermining of the Iron and Steel Trades Confederation. Privatisation followed, then endless cuts and closures. By 2023, Britain produced a mere seven million metric tonnes of steel annually; negligible in global terms.

12.4 Resistance in defeat

The assault on coal was even more calculated. The Ridley Plan, drawn up for the Thatcher government, explicitly aimed to destroy the National Union of Mineworkers and the 1984–5 miners' strike was the decisive confrontation. After it ended, systematic pit closures had a profound and permanent impact on entire communities. Similar patterns played out across engineering, printing, the docks and construction. As manual industrial production and manufacturing were pulled apart, so were the unions that had sustained them.

A loss of confidence was evident as the 1980s wore on. Following the end of the miners' dispute and the print dispute and the docks and steel disputes, in a deeply uncharacteristic suspension of disbelief, the trade union movement swallowed the spurious argument put forward at the 1988 TUC by the then President of the European Union, Jacques Delors, that if only the unions drew up social partnerships with the employers, and supported the single capitalist European market, then milk and honey would flow. It cannot be denied that many of the shackles restricting the unions were not imposed, but mind-forged within the movement itself.

The capacity for resistance was not destroyed, however. Organisations like the Institute of Employment Rights, established in 1989, meticulously catalogued employment legislation and developed alternative proposals. Together with the Campaign for Trade Union Freedom, they maintained knowledge and organisational memory through the worst years and now lead the way with comprehensive manifestos for transformation of the existing labour law framework.

The IER work on this issue from 2016 remains valid and relevant today, but the chance to adopt its proposals was missed in drafting the Employment Rights Bill 2024 (ERB). Strong campaigning and lobbying secured the restoration of several key individual workers' rights that had been stripped away, and many attempts in both Houses of Parliament to weaken the Bill were successfully resisted. Yet, the straitjacket of restrictive labour law largely remains.

No sooner was the Bill published than the unions were proposing that a second, much more substantial version was needed to address the fundamental issues of restoring the democratic rights of unions to bargain by multiemployer sector, to vote for secondary solidarity action and so on. Additionally, it was evident that while re-introducing some valuable individual rights, when the Bill became an Act it still did not address the fundamental fault lines in British labour law as distorted and shaped since 1980. It did not tackle the major problems of the status and the confusion between those who work on a subordinate basis for others, and those genuinely running a business on their own account; low pay and growing inequality as a result of years of deregulation and de-unionisation; insecure jobs affecting the capacity of people who work to have a decent standard of living; the lack of worker voice and lack of worker power, with only a minority of those who work protected by a recognised trade union; the lack of effective remedies, and – as revealed by the P&O Ferries Ltd case when workers were simply fired *en masse* illegally – the failure of our labour law to ensure that employers are required to comply with their legal obligations; and the basic incompatibility of British labour law with international labour standards ratified by the UK.

12.5 Why unions matter for the transformation of Britain

The British labour movement is famously nostalgic. It likes nothing better than to relive past battles, won or lost. Such reminiscences have their place, of course, but it would be a mistake to hark back to a golden age that didn't exist when there are new challenges – such as recruitment in the private service sector – to be faced. Unions have their flaws. Like any institutions they don't always get things right. It would be naive to imagine that the strategy set out in Chapters 8–11 will come about solely as the result of rolling back trade union legislation imposed since the 1980s. But it is also the case that the strategy can't succeed without trade unions having more power and influence. Raising productivity requires capital deepening and skills upgrading. But neither will happen reliably when workers are atomised and employers compete on low wages rather than investment.

Collective bargaining at sector level can enforce the rate for the job, coordinate training, and prevent undercutting. Germany and Italy retained larger manufacturing sectors partly because such agreements enforced training levies and limited precarious contracts. Britain lost these mechanisms.

But collective bargaining is one element among several in rebuilding union strength. Unions matter because they are organisations of production power – they understand work, enforce standards, and can halt output when necessary. They are also institutions that defend workers beyond the wage: health and safety protections, pension rights, equality enforcement, education and training.

Our programme develops conditions for rebuilding union power. Public investment through the proposed Public Investment Bank creates new workplaces that could be unionised with state backing. Procurement rules can favour firms with union recognition and sectoral agreements. Public ownership removes entire sectors from the profit-extracting logic of shareholder capitalism. Capital controls limit employers' ability to play workers in different countries against each other, reducing the race to the bottom on wages and conditions.

12.6 Democracy in practice versus electoral hollowness

Trade unions are democratic institutions, even if they are not perfect, nor have they ever claimed to be. Unions have their share of weaknesses and failures of representation. But at its best, union democracy operates on principles that parliamentary democracy has largely abandoned, that is, continuous participation, direct accountability, and the unity of decision and action. It is worth examining that contrast seriously, because rebuilding union power means rebuilding a culture of active democratic practice that Britain badly needs.

The point to stress is that trade union democracy is necessarily active. Members elect officers and shop stewards, debate policy in branch meetings, vote on industrial action through workplace ballots, hold leadership accountable through annual conferences. Decisions are made collectively through face-to-face debate and argument. When members vote to strike, they implement the decision themselves by withdrawing their labour. When they elect representatives, those shop stewards typically remain workers themselves, experiencing the same conditions as those they represent, and accountable to members between elections in ways that parliamentary representatives are not.

This is democracy as participation and collective decision-making, not as periodic delegation to distant representatives. Union members do not simply vote and hope. They debate, decide and act. The democratic process is direct, continuous rather than episodic, and requires active participation. Power remains with the membership, exercised through structures designed to prevent its capture by bureaucracies or external forces.

The contrast with contemporary parliamentary democracy could hardly be sharper. Voter turnout has declined steadily, and party memberships have collapsed. Politicians campaign on promises but retreat once in office, insulated from effective pressure by centralised party structures and short election cycles. Policy is increasingly made by unelected bodies, such as central banks setting interest rates, regulators determining infrastructure charges, international financial institutions imposing fiscal rules. None of these is accountable to voters.

The electorate has been reduced to passive consumers choosing between pre-packaged options every few years. Between elections, democratic participation is largely absent. Governments claim mandates based on low-vote shares in low-turnout elections, then pursue policies their own voters oppose. When voters express dissatisfaction, they are told to wait for the next election and try again. Meanwhile, financial capital and large corporations maintain continuous access to decision-makers through donations, lobbying and the revolving door between business and government. To cap it all, newspapers, television and other mass media are controlled by huge capitalist conglomerates that regulate the flow of news.

Union democracy, at its best, operates differently. It involves continuous participation: branch meetings where members debate and vote on positions; workplace meetings where immediate issues are discussed and action decided; conferences where delegates from across the union argue over strategy and elect leadership. This creates democratic accountability through practice, not just formal procedures.

When workers vote to strike, the decision is implemented by those who made it. There is no gap between decision and action, no delegation to professionals who might interpret the mandate differently. When shop stewards are elected, they remain workers themselves, experiencing the same conditions as those they represent. If they fail to fight effectively, they can be challenged and replaced immediately, not after years in office.

The anti-trade union assault deliberately targeted this democratic culture. Union education was stripped of political content and turned into technical training. Balloting requirements were designed not to enhance democracy but to make collective action more difficult and costly. Secondary solidarity strikes were banned precisely because they represented workers exercising democratic power beyond the narrow confines of their own workplace and employer. The goal was to fragment collective action and reduce unions to service providers negotiating individual grievances rather than organisations capable of democratic self-governance and collective struggle.

Rebuilding unions means rebuilding this culture of active democracy. It means training members not just in negotiating techniques but in political economy – understanding how production is organised, how profits are extracted, how state policy serves class interests, and how collective action can change all of this. It means democratic structures that genuinely empower members to make decisions and act on them, not simply consultative processes managed by officials.

This dimension is essential for the transformation of the UK outlined in this book. The programme requires sustained democratic pressure to implement and defend against fierce resistance from employers, financial capital and captured state institutions. That pressure cannot come from passive electorates voting every few years and hoping for the best. It can only come from organised workers capable of collective action – striking to enforce demands, occupying workplaces threatened with closure, mobilising communities around investment priorities, holding elected representatives accountable through continuous pressure.

Electoral democracy alone will not deliver transformation. Candidates voted to positions of power usually retreat when confronted by Treasury orthodoxy or City threats. Active democracy can deliver results – workers organised through unions and linked to community organisations, capable of enforcing their collective will through action. This is why rebuilding union power is not simply about improving workplace conditions but about creating the political capacity necessary for national economic transformation.

12.7 The capacity to win

Employer resistance to rebuilt union power will be fierce. Business lobbies will claim that stronger unions destroy competitiveness and flexibility; the press will invoke the 1970s as a cautionary tale; the Treasury will warn of inflation spiralling beyond control. These arguments are not new – they were made against every advance in worker power, from the Factory Acts to the Equal Pay Act, and were as wrong then as they are now.

The real issue is class power, not economic efficiency. Employers and financial capital oppose strong unions because they limit profit extraction through wage suppression and asset-stripping. They prefer fragmented workforces that are incapable of collective resistance. Overcoming that opposition requires confrontation and willingness to use state power to impose a new settlement over their resistance.

The historical record shows collective action can win despite fierce opposition. The Tolpuddle Martyrs were defeated and transported but their struggle inspired generations of workers to organise. The miners lost in 1985 but the issues they fought over – community survival, productive capacity, the right to meaningful work – remain central today. The women at Ford Dagenham and Trico-Folberth won equal pay through persistence against determined employer resistance. The Grunwick workers, though defeated in their immediate aim of union recognition, helped shift wider political terrain on race and union rights, contributing to changes that benefited all workers.

The programme set out in this book creates conditions for rebuilding union power not as precondition that must be achieved before implementation can begin, but in tandem with the process of implementation itself. As public investment creates new productive capacity, new workplaces emerge that can be unionised. As sectoral compacts are negotiated and enforced, collective bargaining coverage expands. As training systems are established, unions gain institutional roles in shaping skills and production standards. As capital controls limit employers' options to offshore production or play workers in different countries against each other, the structural power of labour increases.

Building the political forces capable of seizing these opportunities – unions rebuilt as centres of active democracy, linked to community organisations, connected to wider struggles for public services and sustainable development – is the task ahead. The social coalition required, its material basis in the programme itself, and how it can be built through struggle, is the subject of the next chapter.

13

Building a coalition for transformation

13.1 The vacuum of the 'Big Society'

Not so long ago, food banks were a rarity in Britain. When the Conservative–Liberal Democrat government came to power in 2010 there were 35 places distributing food across the country. Three years later the number had increased to 650 and then doubled again by the end of the decade. In 2024 food banks distributed more than three million food parcels.

Food banks filled the vacuum left by austerity. David Cameron's 'Big Society' promised that volunteerism would compensate for welfare cuts, but this proved to be yet another neoliberal myth. Volunteerism on a shoestring could never replace well-funded public services and professional delivery. George Osborne misleadingly claimed 'we are all in this together' as he pushed through spending cuts, but those at the sharp end knew the reality was different.

Trade unions and community organisations both felt the impact of austerity keenly. As the economy is rebuilt, there is both scope and need for these main representative bodies – of workers in work and of people in society – to work together more closely and revitalise civil society as the driver of social and economic change.

13.2 Communities and unions: rebuilding association on the basis of class

The words community and union express the social and collective nature of human beings and what makes us successful. They go alongside that other vital word: cooperation. Our predecessors spoke of the commonwealth, the riches of the country being shared by all. From the nineteenth century onwards, they used the word socialism. No person is an island – we are interdependent and must cooperate to survive and prosper. We are inherently social creatures.

Association, not separation and individualism, should be a way of life. Breaking up Britain during the past half century through neoliberal policies has involved the breaking of association. The factories and mines that were once the base of sporting, social and community life have been destroyed. Libraries, community centres, youth centres, adult education institutes, village halls have been closed down in their thousands, reducing space and place for people to gather with common purpose.

But the impulse to reconnect is strong. Trade unions in Britain are reaching out to community organisations and community organisations are reaching out to trade unions. This is vital because one of the most debilitating divides is between the concerns and organisations of the workplace and those of the communities in which workers live.

Both unions and community organisations are rooted locally. Individual unions have their regional and national structures. Trade Union Councils bring together unions in localities and often reach out to wider communities. These local TUCs tend to have more power in Wales and Scotland than in England, where they have been marginalised. They should be radically reconstituted to become hubs of local collaboration and coordination.

Community organisations operate in defined neighbourhoods or wider communities of interest. Many focus on campaigns on issues central to us all: health, housing, transport, environment. Others fill gaps in state provision; still others give voice to communities facing cuts and worsening conditions from austerity.

The concerns overlap substantially. Trade unions are membership organisations depending on voluntary engagement. So are most community organisations. Both depend on activity and time freely given for the value of the cause and solidarity. Both are at the centre of democratic practice through elections to office and accountability. This shared basis creates the possibility of genuine collaboration drawing on the common concerns and aspirations of working people.

13.3 Voluntary effort and civic engagement

Around a million people work in charities and community organisations. According to official surveys, more than a third of the population in England are involved in some form of civic participation in a given year; around three-quarters give to charity with about £20 a month being an average donation. The most commonly cited reasons for volunteering are that people want to 'improve things' or 'help people'. The search for solidarity, collective action and association can also be found in trade unionism, with the crucial difference that trade unions are based on the shared aspect of labour, the commonality of employment that shapes the class outlook of their members.

Many community organisations refer to their work to empower people and collectivise campaigning as 'social action'. This is equivalent to what trade unions call campaigning but often has a more sustained presence. According to the Department for Culture, Media and Sport Community Life survey, fifteen per cent of people had been involved in social action in their local area at least once in the previous year.

This voluntary engagement creates similar commitments to egalitarian and democratic practice in both unions and community organisations. Both elect officers and hold them accountable. Both are membership-based rather than top-down. Both depend on face-to-face contact and communication between people, which is essential to organisational success. This stands in sharp contrast to the fragmentation and isolation promoted by social media platforms.

But unions and community organisations need to engage with each other more closely. Union campaigns for rights at work and broader goals – freedom of speech, free health care and education, protection from discrimination – benefit everyone but do not necessarily engage with community organisations in pursuit of their aims. When campaigning and seeking support, unions and community organisations tend to write to the press and MPs. They rarely write to each other to explore effective ways of supporting each other and making wider groups aware of their issues.

13.4 The social forces for transformation

The programme set out in Chapters 8–11 creates the material basis for a coalition of social forces with stakes in breaking with neoliberalism. This coalition cannot be willed into existence through appeals to shared values or abstract solidarity. It emerges from having concrete material interests in the transformation the programme outlines.

The core of this coalition is the transformed working class analysed in earlier chapters. This is no longer the industrial workforce of the 1970s but a fragmented, diverse body: manufacturing workers in what remains of steel, chemicals and engineering; public sector workers in health, education and local government facing pay cuts and collapsing services; young workers trapped in precarious gig economy jobs with no prospect of stable employment or affordable housing; migrant workers exploited at the bottom of labour markets with weak rights and poverty wages. These groups have been divided by modern capitalism – by employment status, by sector, by age, by gender, by origin – but they share material interests in sectoral bargaining that enforces wage floors, public investment that creates stable jobs, and capital controls that prevent employers playing them against each other.

Young workers merit particular attention. They face a uniquely bleak predicament: zero-hours contracts and gig work that pay poverty wages while demanding constant availability; student debt that will take decades to repay; housing costs that make independence impossible, forcing them to live with parents well into their twenties or thirties; and a pervasive sense that no future is available to them. Rates of anxiety, depression and a mental health crisis among young people have escalated dramatically. The programme offers them something concrete: stable jobs with training and progression through sectoral compacts, affordable housing through public investment and controls on speculation, and a future worth planning for rather than endless precarity punctuated by mental health crises.

Layers of professional white-collar workers have been viciously squeezed by austerity and the degradation of public services. Teachers, nurses, social workers, civil servants have witnessed their material conditions worsen dramatically. Real pay has been cut, workloads intensified, autonomy eroded. They see daily the consequences of public underinvestment: schools without supplies, hospitals in crisis, services collapsing. Their stake in transformation is direct: funded services require productive wealth creation, which requires the industrial rebuilding the programme delivers.

Small and medium enterprises, squeezed by lack of credit, unfair competition from monopolies, and dominance of big finance, also have material interest in elements of the programme. Not all will support it – SMEs often rely on low-wage models that collective bargaining threatens – but those in manufacturing supply chains, in construction, in services dependent on stable local economies, can benefit from cheaper energy from public ownership, better infrastructure, and access to patient finance through the PIB rather than commercial lenders.

Finally, the urban poor concentrated in deindustrialised towns and inner-city areas – often reliant on food banks, benefits, and insecure casual work – have stakes in a transformation that creates employment and rebuilds communities.

This coalition of social forces will not form spontaneously. It requires organisation, coordination and institutional mechanisms to bind together diverse groups with different immediate concerns. This is where trade unions and community organisations can play a crucial role.

13.5 Steady rebuilding of institutions

Unions provide the organisational infrastructure for workplace struggle and sectoral bargaining. They connect manufacturing workers in steel to public sector workers in health through Trade Union Councils. They can organise young precariously employed workers alongside older workers with stable employment. They provide democratic structures through which diverse groups can debate strategy and coordinate action.

Community organisations provide the infrastructure for organising outside the workplace. Tenant groups, food banks, environmental campaigns, pensioner organisations – all connect people around shared concerns beyond employment. They mobilise around housing, transport, services, environment. They create spaces for democratic participation, where unions have little presence.

The programme for reindustrialisation can quickly begin to deliver concrete material benefits to different groups. A public-sector worker in Newcastle benefits when steel sector compacts create jobs and tax revenues; a young worker in Manchester benefits from training obligations; a deindustrialised community in South Wales benefits from public investment; an SME in manufacturing benefits from stable supply chains and infrastructure investment; community organisations see their campaigns for better transport and housing materialise in practice.

But these institutions alone are insufficient. The coalition requires political expression capable of wielding state power to implement the programme against fierce resistance. The institutional links between workplace and community, between unions and tenant groups, between political parties and grassroots campaigns matter because they create organised force capable of sustaining the programme under assault.

The alternative to this difficult struggle is continued decline. The productive base is too weak, external dependence too great, the climate crisis too urgent. Building the coalition and fighting for its political expression is necessary work.

This book has laid out what transformation requires economically, institutionally and politically. But programmes do not implement themselves and coalitions do not hold together by goodwill alone. What ultimately determines whether a strategy of this kind succeeds or fails is whether the social forces behind it can exercise real power. Not simply electoral power, which capital has repeatedly shown it can contain, but the practical capacity to implement democratic decisions against organised resistance. That capacity is what we mean by sovereignty. What it requires in practice, and why recovering it is the central political task of our time, is the subject of the final chapter.

14
National sovereignty and active democracy

14.1 June 2016 and what it meant

The day 23 June 2016 was a beautiful summer's day in Britain. As people went to vote in the EU referendum, opinion polls suggested that by a narrow margin voters would decide – as they had in 1975 – to remain in the EU. Instead, as night wore on and the votes were counted, something seismic was taking place. On an enormous turnout, fifty-two per cent of those who voted opted for Britain to leave. The vote for Brexit was highest in industrial heartlands blighted by manufacturing collapse and austerity – South Wales, the North East, parts of the Midlands. The vote to remain was strongest in London and university towns, the more prosperous parts of Britain. Many students saw the referendum as a choice between chauvinism and internationalism, with membership of the EU providing opportunities to travel and to study abroad. The fact that the campaign to leave was dominated by politicians of the right only served to sharpen these concerns.

Scepticism about the EU was once widespread, stretching back to Prime Minister Clement Attlee's reluctance to join the European Coal and Steel Community. Tony

Benn and other socialist Labour MPs, many trade unions, and the TUC itself had made the left-wing case against European integration. The critique proved right. The EU was built on neoliberal principles enshrined in its Treaties. The single market's four spurious freedoms for goods, services, labour and capital prevented democratic interference with market forces; competition law severely restricted state aid; public procurement required tendering across the Union; Maastricht criteria restricted fiscal deficits. These were not accidental features but its core architecture.

The Brexit vote expressed legitimate dislike for this neoliberal project but there was also something deeper going on. The British working class found an opportunity to declare its deep anger at the ruling elite that had shaped the country's fortunes for decades. 'Take Back Control' resonated because millions had lost control over jobs, communities and economic futures.

What happened next was not what was wanted. The Tories had no plan other than fantasies of aggressive commercial Britain buccaneering across the oceans. Instead of using the policy space that leaving the EU created, they continued with neoliberal orthodoxy and wasted the opportunity.

Brexit by itself solved nothing. But it removed obstacles. Britain is no longer bound by EU single-market disciplines on state aid and capital mobility. The programme in Chapters 8–11 uses that space – capital controls, sectoral compacts, public ownership, procurement favouring domestic production. The task is implementation, which hinges on the reassertion of popular and national sovereignty. Sovereignty is a necessary precondition of policy. Without control over legislation, state aid, procurement, and capital movements, the strategy set out in this book would be impossible.

It is also impossible to implement the strategy without control of the central levers of the state, above all its legislative authority and administrative capacity, with willingness to wield both against determined resistance. Public investment, industrial planning, capital controls, energy transformation and labour market reform all depend on state power. Social mobilisation, trade union strength and community organisations are essential, but they are not substitutes for holding office.

None of this will happen without an election victory that brings parliamentary control. However broad the coalition behind economic renewal, it must translate into a governing majority capable of passing legislation and sustaining it under pressure. Electoral victory is not sufficient on its own, but without it the programme remains aspirational. The task is therefore to build political forces capable of winning office and using it decisively.

Once in office, the early period matters most because then opposition is least coordinated, legitimacy is highest, and the institutional terrain can be reshaped before resistance hardens. This window must be used to lock in the legal and institutional framework on which everything else depends, including emergency investment authorisations, public ownership of strategic infrastructure, reformed procurement and planning rules, new delivery bodies with clear statutory mandates, and capital account measures ready for activation. Delay concedes ground to those whose interests are threatened.

Seizing that window requires not just institutional preparation but political clarity about the exercise of power. That clarity begins with a question that divides left from right on the terrain of national sovereignty: in whose interests is the nation run?

14.2 Popular sovereignty and democracy

The nation can be understood in two radically different ways and many political activists in Britain confuse the two. One is chauvinist, an empty jingoism pretending a superiority to everybody else. The other, a socialist understanding of the importance of the nation, is the one we reflect and seek to promote in this book. This chapter makes the progressive argument for a re-invigorated nation state and a return of the understanding of the importance of our nation and active citizenship from a socialist perspective.

Popular sovereignty is the practical capacity to formulate and implement democratic decisions – the ability to make the popular will effective. That capacity depends on institutions that make it real: voice and power at work, in the neighbourhood, in the city, in the region, in the country. It is democracy as active participation, not passive voting every few years.

As Chapter 12 established, union democracy involves continuous participation – branch meetings where workers debate and decide, workplace ballots that members implement themselves, shop stewards subject to immediate recall. This is democracy with teeth. The same principle applies beyond the workplace. Community organisations must have power to shape planning, demand investment, challenge developments benefiting speculators. Reconstituted local authorities need genuine budgets and autonomy. Regional development agencies need decision-making powers and must be accountable to democratic structures rather than business elites. They should be able to coordinate investment, connect firms to supply chains, ensure training matches local needs, thus reversing the hyper-centralisation of the British state.

Nationally, the central state must implement economic programmes overcoming objections from unaccountable financial capital. Parliamentary democracy should respond to voters rather than being captured by lobbying. Unelected institutions, such as Treasury bureaucrats determining fiscal rules, and the Bank of England setting interest rates shaping employment, must be brought under democratic control. Monetary and fiscal rules are political choices that distribute income, risk and power across society. Democratic control means revising statutory mandates and accountability structures so that macroeconomic policy serves productive investment and employment rather than the interests of a tiny elite.

Neoliberalism has systematically sought to reduce the democratic capacity of citizens in the UK. Turnout in elections declines as people recognise that voting changes little. Politicians campaign on promises but retreat once in office citing market constraints. Between elections, participation ceases. Crucial decisions are made by bodies accountable to no one.

Breaking this deadlock requires institutions that enable continuous democratic participation, such as revitalised trade unions and community organisations. The social coalition required to implement the programme of transformation can draw strength from their functioning. Without them, diverse social forces remain fragmented; with them, popular sovereignty can become the political basis for transformation and foundation of national sovereignty itself.

But institutional change alone is insufficient. Two generations of workers have internalised the values of the market, shaped into passive consumers rather than active citizens, their collective solidarities eroded from within as much as attacked from without. It therefore followed that patriotism became falsely equated with negative chauvinism, and democracy was identified with unelected EU Commissioners. National planning and coordination in industry, transport, utilities, food production and welfare services was condemned as centralist. Only the market would save us, we were told. No one should get in its way.

As deregulated markets reduced people to competing units of consumption, collective rights gave way to individual liberties and identity claims. Class, and its organised expression in trade unions and community institutions, came to seem outdated. With the economic argument conceded to neoliberalism, political activism fragmented into a proliferation of single-issue campaigns. The Enlightenment conviction in shared humanity and collective reason was displaced by a politics of particular identities and specific grievances, each legitimate in itself but incapable alone of challenging the system that produced them.

14.3 National sovereignty and citizenship

National sovereignty, properly understood, is popular sovereignty expressed at the level of the nation. It rests on the capacity to decide how resources are generated, allocated and invested, and to defend those decisions against external economic coercion. It means that the nation is controlled democratically by working people rather than by industrial and financial capital, and certainly not by foreign powers. It answers who decides how the nation's productive capacity is used, and how does the nation position itself internationally. It makes clear the social interests that dictate these answers.

This is class politics taking national form. Workers need sovereign control over economic policy to implement the programme outlined in this book. That sovereignty must be exercised in favour of working people and the poor, against capital. It stands opposed to capital's globalisation – freedom from democratic constraint, ability to relocate production wherever wages are lowest, escape regulation through jurisdictional arbitrage. It also stands opposed to aggressive capitalist expansionism overseas that leads to oppression over other people.

National sovereignty is not nationalism. This distinction matters fundamentally. Nationalism in its reactionary form traffics in ethnic identity, cultural superiority, exclusion of outsiders. It serves capital by dividing workers along national lines. It wraps itself in the Union Jack, is hostile to anyone not born British, it offers a symbolic belonging to a mythical national community, while stripping workers and the poor from material power.

National sovereignty as used here rests entirely on popular sovereignty described above. The nation becomes sovereign when working people exercise democratic control through institutions at every level. In the old language of the workers' movement, the aim is to make the nation speak the language of the working class and the poor, not of capitalists and the rich. That is sovereignty as workers' power.

This kind of sovereignty is the foundation of true internationalism, which supports workers everywhere rather than pitting national workforces against each other. It means backing struggles for decent wages and conditions in other countries. It also means opposing imperialism – Britain's historic role internationally but also more recently as a junior partner to US global power.

For centuries, the British ruling class advanced the Empire when it served capital accumulation, then abandoned it once direct rule became too costly and national liberation movements gained strength. It backed industry when manufacturing capital dominated the ruling bloc, then oversaw deindustrialisation as financial capital rose to power. Its success has always come from serving the leading fractions of capital – over the past five decades, chiefly those of finance based in the City of London. Britain's imperial legacy now persists through financial networks: the City extracts wealth from developing countries via debt servicing, capital flight through tax havens, and corporate tax avoidance by UK-based firms.

True internationalism means supporting liberation struggles everywhere while rejecting Britain's role as junior partner enforcing US hegemony. It means opposing military interventions dressed as humanitarian missions. It means solidarity with workers and progressive governments resisting US pressure and blackmail. The task is extending that internationalist solidarity to include struggle within Britain itself – freeing the country from internal domination by big business and finance, building an economy serving working people, building sufficient political power to enable us to be genuinely internationalist.

This new programme we propose draws on the best traditions of the British working class and embodies that solidarity in practice. To be sure, there are many unsavoury, even shameful episodes in Britain's history, of which the legacy of colonialism is the most enduring. The story of the past is not just of kings crowned, queens beheaded, and battles won. But while not downplaying the bad, it is also important to celebrate the good.

Britain was shaped by the democratic and radical traditions of the Medieval guilds and conventicles, and by the dissenting, non-conformist churches. It is the story of science, technology and the secular consciousness that flowed from the first Industrial Revolution and Enlightenment. It is the tradition of progressive liberties, non-sectarianism, free speech and respect. It is a country with a majority that has consistently rejected racism and discrimination, where fascist parties have not achieved power or significant influence as they have in most other European countries. And it is a country in which the ultra-right will not find it easy to rise in this vacuum and claim they speak for us.

Black and minority ethnic scholars and community activists and artists have also shaped Britain in so many important ways. There is a long and rich tradition in this regard, from Olaudah Equiano the great abolitionist, through William Cuffay the Chartist leader to thousands of others in our own times.

Ultimately, Britain is only its workers and its natural resources. When combined, they create all wealth. To say the nation has no place in the new world order, is to say workers do not have a place. British workers built the first trade unions, created the first Industrial Revolution, and their struggles in various forms shaped many of our country's great arts and institutions.

Capital controls prevent British firms exploiting cheap labour overseas while undermining wages at home. They also prevent financial markets from disciplining democratic decisions through capital flight and speculative attacks on the currency or public debt. An immigration policy that is aligned with training systems and wage floors prevents employers using migrant labour to undercut pay. Workers are welcomed on terms of genuine solidarity – equal pay for equal work, full union rights, clear pathways to settlement. And asylum seekers are defended without qualification.

Young people rightly recoil from nationalism as they've experienced it with the rise of the authoritarian right. But what they are offered here in these proposals is sovereignty as democratic expression of workers of all backgrounds to control their economic future together. It is a stance that derives from the proud history of the British working class that stood against invading Iraq, and stands today for Palestine, and strongly opposes propping up oppressive regimes abroad, and extracting wealth from former colonies through City financial networks.

This is also the basis on which to understand citizenship today. Under neoliberalism, citizenship has become hollow, merely a legal status granting passport-holding, voting rights, access to services. It is passive, individualistic, transactional. True citizenship means active contribution to the common good through work, organising, participation in democratic institutions. It is defined by what people do – their labour, solidarity, active engagement in shaping society – not by documents or ethnic origin.

This understanding naturally includes legal immigrants. Workers from Poland or Pakistan labouring in British factories or hospitals, joining a union, participating in community campaigns can become citizens in this meaningful sense. They contribute to wealth creation, participate in democratic struggles, have material stake in the transformation of the country as well as the obligations this entails.

14.4 Environmental sovereignty and climate justice

Sovereignty also means capacity to address environmental and climate crisis on terms serving working people rather than corporate interests. International cooperation will be vital if global warming is to be tackled successfully because greenhouse gas emissions know no borders. Yet without sovereignty over economic policy, climate action becomes impossible. Market mechanisms have manifestly failed.

And so, sovereignty means implementing climate policy against determined corporate resistance. It requires public ownership of energy systems enabling rapid decarbonisation unconstrained by shareholder profit demands. It requires industrial strategy creating climate jobs – manufacturing solar panels, wind turbines, heat pumps, electric vehicles domestically rather than importing them and offshoring both emissions and employment. It requires capital controls preventing firms from relocating rather than reducing emissions.

Our programme integrates climate action with industrial rebuilding. Public investment in electricity generation, grid expansion, building retrofit, transport electrification creates employment while reducing emissions. Sectoral compacts tie decarbonisation targets directly to training programmes and job guarantees, ensuring workers benefit materially from transition. This embodies environmental justice: workers and communities don't bear transition costs while capital escapes.

Climate action challenges powerful interests with enormous resources. Fossil fuel companies resist transition through lobbying and threats of economic disruption. Financial institutions oppose regulation threatening stranded assets worth trillions. Multinational corporations demand freedom to locate production wherever emissions standards are weakest.

Overcoming this requires state power wielded democratically – direct public investment, ownership, and regulation enforced through popular mobilisation. Young people's climate activism has been met with corporate greenwashing substituting for action because sovereignty remains with those benefiting from the existing system. Transferring it to working people creates genuine possibility of climate action matching scientific necessity.

14.5 Fighting for sovereignty

National mobilisation on the scale required has historical precedent. After the Second World War, Britain was rebuilt from devastation through deliberate transformation. For those who had endured Depression before fighting fascism, national solidarity to tackle poverty emerged from bitter experience. The NHS was founded by rejecting market provision; major industries were nationalised; full employment became explicit policy; council housing was built at massive scale.

This required intense political struggle. Unions rebuilt during wartime demanded fundamental change. Both major parties were forced to accept a new settlement through working-class mobilisation, and that involved conflict, strikes, confrontation – not consensus.

More recently, Covid demonstrated that rapid mobilisation remains possible when crisis is recognised as urgent. The pandemic revealed who keeps society functioning: health workers, rail and transport workers, civil servants, postal workers, delivery drivers, shop workers. Society functions because all workers contribute essential parts through integrated, reciprocal activity. Yet once crisis passed, recognition evaporated. Health workers faced renewed pay cuts and care workers remained on poverty wages. The demonstrated capacity for mobilisation was not sustained.

The transformation outlined here requires similar mobilisation but sustained over years, pursued as deliberate reconstruction rather than emergency response. The capacity to implement democratic decisions will not be granted voluntarily. It must be won through sustained struggle. Financial capital, multinational corporations, the Treasury, captured regulators, right-wing media will resist ferociously. They will deploy familiar arguments: transformation is impossible, unaffordable, dangerous. They will threaten capital flight, predict collapse, invoke international obligations.

These are political weapons defending class interests. Overcoming them requires building institutions of popular sovereignty capable of sustaining organised pressure. It requires unions strong enough to strike effectively, occupy workplaces, enforce sectoral agreements. It requires community organisations mobilising around investment, challenging planning decisions, demanding accountability. It requires political organisation forcing elected representatives to choose: implement transformation or face organised opposition.

Programmes and agents of change develop together through struggle. Workers recognise their stake in sectoral compacts when wages rise, then organise to defend victories. Communities see investment materialising, then mobilise to shape it. Young people find stable employment in green industries, then join unions. Women gain equal pay through collective bargaining, then strengthen organisation. Each success creates foundation for further advance.

This is sovereignty as democratic capacity built through practical struggle. It is concrete power embodied in institutions that stands as alternative to neoliberalism's hollow democracy: passive voting followed by rule by unelected technocrats.

Britain has the right to determine its own destiny, as do all countries. That's why self-determination is so essential to the socialist project internationally. We have the right to arrange our life as we see fit, without, of course, trampling on the rights of other nations as capitalist Britain has so brutally done in the past. We believe in a world of peacefully co-existing nations.

Preparation is therefore not optional. Capital controls must be drafted in advance, with legislative frameworks ready and enforcement mechanisms identified. The Bank of England's mandate must be revised by statute to support productive investment, with explicit authority to support gilt markets and provide liquidity to the Public Investment Bank. Legislation must be tightly written to minimise discretion and obstruction, with statutory duties aligned directly to programme objectives. Regulatory bodies must be reoriented from procedural gatekeeping towards delivery, with performance measured against output rather than process.

Financial resistance requires specific responses. When capital threatens flight, controls close the channels. When bond markets test yields, the Bank of England acts as backstop through purchases and repo operations, with public communication that makes clear the state cannot be forced into default by speculation. When commercial lenders withdraw credit or demand prohibitive rates, the Public Investment Bank steps in as lender on published terms, breaking the private sector's pricing power over long-term finance. These are not theoretical possibilities but operational requirements, and they must be ready before resistance begins.

The programme itself is a mechanism of political mobilisation. Organising around abstract principles produces temporary campaigns that dissipate when immediate demands are met or defeated. Organising around a concrete programme that delivers material improvements in employment, wages, energy costs, housing and public services creates an expanding constituency with a direct stake in defending and extending transformation. New factories employ workers who join unions and vote to protect their jobs. Apprenticeships create skilled workers whose careers depend on the programme continuing. Lower energy bills from public ownership generate broad household support. This is not cynical vote-buying but the material basis of class politics. People defend what materially improves their lives.

Legitimacy under pressure depends on visible results. Disruption is inevitable when an economy is restructured. The question is whether costs are distributed fairly and benefits arrive quickly enough to maintain support. Progress must be measured in concrete terms, such as manufacturing employment growth, volumes of Public Investment Bank lending, completed grid connections, extended sectoral bargaining coverage, increased training throughput, rising real wages. These are the proof points.

The transformation will face moments of acute crisis. Markets will test the government's resolve, probably early. Inflation may rise temporarily as capacity lags demand. International partners will apply pressure through trade threats or institutional channels. Media will amplify every difficulty. The response in each case must be decisive, acting with prepared measures, explaining the transition clearly, maintaining course rather than retreating, and accelerating delivery to demonstrate competence. Governments that hold firm and show results shift the policy terrain.

The choice facing Britain is not between technocracy and mobilisation, or between markets and planning. It is between continued decline under a form of capitalism that concentrates wealth and power, while destroying productive capacity, and a deliberate effort to rebuild that capacity under democratic control by workers and the broad majority. To achieve that, it is necessary to take control over key mechanisms of the state and use them against the interests that currently command them.

The specific political vehicle that will achieve this transformation cannot be fixed in advance. What can be stated are the requirements. The vehicle must be capable of winning a parliamentary majority; it must be accountable to organised workers and communities rather than financial donors; and its leadership must understand that implementation requires confrontation with capital, not accommodation. Britain's electoral geography makes Labour the most plausible terrain, but only if it breaks decisively with Treasury orthodoxy and City influence. Whether that break comes through internal transformation or external pressure remains open. The programme provides the framework; building the political force to carry it through is the task facing unions, community organisations and socialist activists.

It is a formidable challenge, but an independent Britain putting its people before profit and living in peace with the world is a realistic prospect. A self-reliant, high-tech, green, industrial economy is within our grasp.

We are citizens, not subjects, and we must be active citizens. The financiers and corporations who have political power, have no allegiance to our country, nor do they care for the planet. The destiny of the nation is only in the hands of all who work here. It was our great revolutionary poet William Blake who wrote that 'no bird can fly too high that flies with its own wings'.

Notes and References

The broader analysis drew generally on several sources, including the following:

Bank of England (2025). Unlocking growth: what can the literature tell us about what's holding back high-growth firms? https://www.bankofengland.co.uk/bank-overground/2025/unlocking-growth-what-can-the-literature-tell-us-about-whats-holding-back-high-growth-firms?utm_source=chatgpt.com

Brown, R., Linares-Zegarra, J. M. and J. O. S. Wilson (2018). An empirical examination of discouraged borrowers in the UK, ERC Research Paper 69. https://www.enterpriseresearch.ac.uk/wp-content/uploads/2018/05/ERC-ResPap69-BrownLinares-ZegarraWilson.pdf

Brown, R., Linares-Zegarra, J. M. and J. O. S. Wilson (2022). 'Innovation and Borrower Discouragement in SMEs', *Small Business Economics* 59(4), 1489–1517.

Buller, A., Lawrence, M., Hager, S. B. and J. Baines (2020). Commoning the Company, Common Wealth. https://openaccess.city.ac.uk/id/eprint/30014/

Cabinet Office (2025). Statistical bulletin – Civil Service Statistics: 2025, Accredited official statistics. https://www.gov.uk/government/statistics/civil-service-statistics-2025/statistical-bulletin-civil-service-statistics-2025

Climate Change Committee (2025). Progress in reducing emissions – 2025 report to Parliament. https://www.theccc.org.uk/publication/progress-in-reducing-emissions-2025-report-to-parliament

Department for Energy Security and Net Zero (2023). The role of gas storage and other forms of flexibility in security of supply. https://assets.publishing.service.gov.uk/media/656fae319462260721c56977/gas-storage-and-flexibility-update.pdf

Department for Energy Security and Net Zero (2025). UK energy in brief 2025. https://www.gov.uk/government/statistics/uk-energy-in-brief-2025

Department for Energy Security and Net Zero (2025). Framework document between the Department for Energy Security and Net Zero and National Energy System Operator. https://assets.publishing.service.gov.uk/media/677b9ba82d00f0ee1996d825/neso-framework-document.pdf

Department for Transport (2024). Transport Statistics Great Britain: 2023 Freight. https://www.gov.uk/government/statistics/transport-statistics-great-britain-2024/transport-statistics-great-britain-2023-freight

Department for Transport (2025). Draft Road Investment Strategy 3. https://assets.publishing.service.gov.uk/media/68ca9c35995dfd01bff0bfec/draft-ris-3.pdf

Department of Education (2022). Opportunities and challenges for improving labour market information on skills. Report by the Skills and Productivity Board (Feb 2022). https://www.gov.uk/government/publications/opportunities-and-challenges-of-improving-labour-market-information

FSB (2023). Revised Policy Recommendations to Address Structural Vulnerabilities from Liquidity Mismatch in Open-Ended Funds. https://www.fsb.org/2023/12/revised-policy-recommendations-to-address-structural-vulnerabilities-from-liquidity-mismatch-in-open-ended-funds

Ghosh, A. and Qureshi, M (2016). What is in a name? That which we call capital controls, IMF Working Paper /16/25.

Gmyrek, P., Berg, J. and Bescond, D. (2023). Generative AI and jobs: A global analysis of potential effects on job quantity and quality, ILO Working Paper 96 (Geneva, ILO). https://doi.org/10.54394/ FHEM8239

HM Revenue & Customs (2024). PAYE and corporate tax receipts from the banking sector. https://www.gov.uk/govern

ment/statistics/paye-and-corporate-tax-receipts-from-the-bank ing-sector-2024/paye-and-corporate-tax-receipts-from-the -banking-sector-2024

Hutton, G., Panjwani, A. and Ward, M. (2024). Financial services in the UK, Commons Library Research Briefing No. 6193. https://researchbriefings.files.parliament.uk/documents /SN06193/SN06193.pdf

IOSCO (2025). Revised Recommendations for Liquidity Risk Management for Collective Investment Schemes. https://www.iosco.org/library/pubdocs/pdf/IOSCOPD798.pdf

Khan, S., Li, B. and Zhao, Y. (2025). Pension reform and stock market development, IMF Working Paper Series 25/49. https://doi.org/10.5089/9798229002318.001

Lapavitsas C. and EReNSEP Collective (2023). *The State Of Capitalism: Economy, Society, and Hegemony*, London: Verso.

National Highways (2022). Strategic Road Network Initial Report 2025–30. https://nationalhighways.co.uk/media/3v2nq see/cre22_0102-srn-initial-report-2025-2030_vn-updated.pdf

OECD (2024). Higher technical education in England, United Kingdom: Insights from selected international experience, OECD Reviews of Vocational Education and Training, OECD Publishing, Paris. https://doi.org/10.1787/7c00dff7-en.

Ofgem (2025). RIIO-3 draft determinations for the electricity transmission, Gas Distribution and Gas Transmission sectors. https://www.ofgem.gov.uk/consultation/riio-3-draft-deter minations-electricity-transmission-gas-distribution-and-gas-transmission-sectors

Ofwat (2024). UK government priorities and our 2024 price review final determinations. https://www.ofwat.gov.uk/wp -content/uploads/2024/12/UK-Government-priorities-and-our -2024-price-review-final-determinations.pdf

ONS (2023), Ownership of UK Quoted Shares: 2022. https://www.ons.gov.uk/economy/investmentspensionsandtrusts/bul letins/ownershipofukquotedshares/2022

ONS (2024). UK Balance of Payments, The Pink Book: 2024. https://www.ons.gov.uk/economy/nationalaccounts/balanceof payments/bulletins/unitedkingdombalanceofpaymentsthepink book/2024

ONS (2025). Labour market in the regions of the UK, Labour Force Survey (August 2025 release). https://www.ons.gov.uk/releases/labourmarketintheregionsoftheukaugust2025

Ostry, J. (2023). The IMF's journey on capital controls: What is the destination?, *Oxford Review of Economic Policy*, 2023, 39, 325–32. https://doi.org/10.1093/oxrep/grad005

Public and Commercial Services Union (2025). The need for tax justice. https://mypcs.my.salesforce.com/sfc/p/#1t000000oksc/a/Sl00000Bru5m/BCiu7dIjs9b.towSm1Wfcl45lTmQg.XwsYVvqm2RK5I

Rail Maritime and Transport Union (2025). Great British Railways and the Productivity Puzzle. https://www.rmt.org.uk/news/public-document-library/great-british-railways-and-the-productivity-puzzle-rmt-report/?preview=true

Rhodes, C., Hough, D. and L. Butcher (2014). Privatisation, Research Paper 14/61, House of Commons Library. https://researchbriefings.files.parliament.uk/documents/RP14-61/RP14-61.pdf

UK Steel (2024). UK CBAM: Creating a level playing field with robust carbon leakage protection. https://www.uksteel.org/uk-carbon-border-adjustment-mechanism-1

UNIDO (2025). Manufacturing production and trade, resilient manufacturing defies economic challenges, Quarterly Report Q1 2025. https://stat.unido.org/portal/storage/file/publications/qiip/World_Manufacturing_Production_2025_Q1.pdf

Unite the Union (2025). Energy Profiteering. https://www.unitetheunion.org/media/b2kldhmg/profiteering-doc-october-30-fv.pdf

Ward, M. (2025). Foreign direct investment statistics, Research Briefing CBP 8534, House of Commons Library. https://commonslibrary.parliament.uk/research-briefings/cbp-8534/

World Bank (2023). Making public investment work for growth. https://documents1.worldbank.org/curated/en/099408408092319382/pdf/IDU0301a3e760c732046e509d3106e81810de4b9.pdf

World Trade Organization (2012). Agreement on Government Procurement 2012. https://www.wto.org/english/docs_e/legal_e/rev-gpr-94_01_e.pdf

Further notes on the figures

Figure 3.1 Public sector current receipts (JW2O), National accounts taxes (GCSU), Total managed expenditure (KX5Q).

Figure 3.2 Public sector net borrowing, J5II.

Figure 3.3 PS: Net Debt (excluding public sector banks) as a percentage of GDP: NSA. Before 1983, only Q1 for each year is recorded.

Figure 3.4 Weekly Reporting was used instead of the Balance Sheet Data as the latter is only available since 2013. APF Data (*'Weekly amounts outstanding of Central Bank sterling loan to Asset Purchase Facility total (in sterling millions) not seasonally adjusted RPWZ4TM')* is only available since September 2013. As an estimate of APF before September 2013 *('Weekly stock of holdings of gilts by the Bank of England's asset purchase facility (in sterling millions) YWWB9T9'*) were used.

Figure 4.1 Output per worker is shown in international dollars, adjusted for Purchasing Power Parity (PPP), accounting for different price levels across countries, allowing for a more accurate comparison of real economic productivity.

Figure 4.2 Data from the OECD was used for the sectoral percentage of total Gross Fixed Capital Formation, and data from the Word Bank was used for Gross Fixed Capital Formation as a percentage of GDP.

Figure 4.3 Adjusted savings, net national savings (% of GNI): Net national savings are equal to gross national savings less the value of consumption of fixed capital. This indicator is expressed as a percentage of Gross National Income (GNI), which is the total income earned by all residents within an economic territory during an accounting period.

Figure 4.4 Credit is provided by all sectors in the UK, not only banking.

Figure 6.3 Note that no data for bottom 50 is available earlier.

Figure 6.5 Note that British citizens are excluded in the figure.

Table 8.1 Share of GDP data for all countries based on World Bank. https://data.worldbank.org/indicator/NV.IND.MANF.ZS. Data on the UK has been collected using: https://www.ons.gov.uk/employmentandlabourmarket/peopleinwork/employmentandemployeetypes/timeseries/jwr7/lms; Italian data comes from https://www.istat.it/storage/rapporto-annuale

/2023/Rapporto-Annuale-2023.pdf and German data can be found under https://www.destatis.de/EN/Themes/Economic-Sectors-Enterprises/Industry-Manufacturing/_node.html#sprg475770

Glossary

Asset Purchase Facility (APF)
A programme of the Bank of England designed to purchase financial assets – principally government and corporate bonds – to inject liquidity into the economy and support monetary policy objectives.

Austerity
A fiscal policy strategy aimed at reducing government deficits through spending cuts, tax increases, or both, usually implemented during periods of elevated public debt.

Bonds
Debt instruments issued by governments, corporations, or other entities to raise capital, entitling holders to interest payments ('coupons') and the repayment of principal at maturity.

Capacity
The maximum potential output an economy, industry, or enterprise can achieve using its existing resources and technology.

Capital Controls
Regulatory measures imposed by governments to restrict or manage cross-border movements of capital, often to preserve financial stability or influence exchange rates.

Capital Deepening
An increase in the amount of capital (such as machinery or infrastructure) available per worker, commonly associated with productivity growth.

Carbon Border Adjustment Mechanism (CBAM)
A European Union policy designed to put a price on the carbon emissions embedded in certain imported goods, aiming to prevent carbon leakage and ensure a level playing field between domestic and foreign producers.

Current Account
A component of the Balance of Payments that records trade in goods and services, income from abroad, and net current transfers.

Electric Vehicle (EV)
A vehicle powered wholly or partially by electric batteries instead of an internal combustion engine.

Financialisation
The growing dominance of financial markets, motives, and institutions in economic activity, often leading to profit generation through financial rather than productive means.

Financial Account
The section of the balance of payments that tracks cross-border capital flows, including foreign direct investment, portfolio investment, and reserve changes.

Financial Liberalisation
The process of deregulating financial markets and capital flows to enhance market efficiency, competition, and integration.

Fiscal Policy
Government policy concerning taxation and public expenditure designed to influence macroeconomic conditions such as growth, employment and inflation.

Financial Transaction Tax (FTT)
A tax levied on specific types of financial transactions, such as trades in shares, bonds, or derivatives, often intended to discourage speculation or generate revenue.

Foreign Direct Investment (FDI)
Long-term investment made by a resident of one economy in the business interests of another, typically implying managerial control or lasting influence.

Gilts
UK government bonds issued by HM Treasury to finance public borrowing and debt management.

Global Credit Bubble
A period characterised by excessive global credit expansion and speculative borrowing, often preceding financial instability or crisis.

Global Financial Crisis (GFC), or Great Crisis of 2007–9
The severe worldwide financial crash and economic downturn of 2007–9, triggered by the collapse of the US housing market and systemic failures in global banking.

Globalisation
The process of increasing interconnection and integration of economies, societies, and cultures through production, trade, finance, migration, and technology.

Gold Standard
A monetary system under which the value of a currency is directly linked to a specified quantity of gold.

Gross Domestic Product (GDP)
The total market value of all final goods and services produced within a country's borders in a specific period, used as a primary measure of economic activity.

Gross National Income (GNI)
The total income earned by a nation's residents and businesses, including net income from abroad.

Gross National Savings
The portion of national income that is saved by households, businesses, and the government, rather than spent on consumption.

Gross Value Added (GVA)
A measure of the value of goods and services produced in an economy, industry, or sector, net of intermediate inputs.

Hegemon
A dominant state or actor that exercises leadership or control over others within a regional or global order.

Looser Fiscal and Monetary Policy
A combination of expansionary fiscal measures (higher spending or lower taxes) and accommodative monetary policy (lower interest rates or asset purchases) to stimulate economic activity.

Monetary Policy
The set of actions by a central bank to regulate the money supply and interest rates to achieve macroeconomic stability, including price stability and employment.

National Debt
The cumulative total of a government's outstanding debt resulting from past budget deficits.

National Deficit
The annual shortfall that occurs when a government's expenditures exceed its revenues within a fiscal year.

National Insurance (NI)
A UK system of compulsory contributions from workers and employers used to fund social benefits such as pensions and unemployment support.

Neoliberalism
An economic and political philosophy favouring market liberalisation, deregulation, privatisation, and reduced state intervention in the economy.

Office for Budget Responsibility (OBR)
An independent UK public body that analyses and forecasts public finances, providing oversight of fiscal policy.

Organisation for Economic Co-operation and Development (OECD)
An intergovernmental organisation that promotes economic growth, policy coordination, and best practices among advanced and emerging economies.

Pay As You Earn (PAYE)
The UK system by which employers deduct income tax directly from employees' wages before payment.

Populism
A political approach that claims to represent the common people against perceived elites, often characterised by anti-establishment and nationalist rhetoric.

Precarity
A condition of economic and social insecurity arising from unstable employment, low income, or inadequate social protection.

Productivity of Labour
The amount of output produced per unit of labour input, usually measured per worker or per hour worked.

Quantitative Easing (QE)
An unconventional monetary policy through which a central bank purchases financial assets to increase liquidity and reduce long-term interest rates.

Quantitative Tightening (QT)
The process by which a central bank reduces its balance sheet by selling assets or allowing them to mature, tightening liquidity conditions.

Recession
A period of sustained economic decline, typically defined as two or more consecutive quarters of negative GDP growth.

Shadow Banking
Financial intermediation that occurs outside the traditional banking system, involving entities and activities not subject to standard regulatory oversight.

Subprime Mortgage Crisis
The 2007–9 financial collapse triggered by the proliferation of high-risk mortgage lending and the securitisation of subprime loans, leading to widespread banking failures.

Total Managed Expenditure (TME)
The UK government's comprehensive measure of public spending, encompassing departmental and annually managed expenditures.

Trade Deficit
A situation in which the value of a country's imports of goods and services exceeds its exports.

Trade Surpluses
A condition in which a country's exports of goods and services exceed its imports, resulting in a positive trade balance.

Trickle-Down Economics
An economic theory suggesting that benefits provided to high-income individuals or corporations will eventually stimulate growth and benefit the wider economy.

Index

Figures are in *italics* and tables are in **bold**.